Get Your Dating Game On

PERSONAL ADS

Get Your Dating Game On

A Field Guide to Playing for Kicks or for Keeps

Jennifer Worick

LAUREL GLEN
San Diego, California

Laurel Glen Publishing
An imprint of the Advantage Publishers Group
5880 Oberlin Drive, San Diego, CA 92121-4794
www.laurelglenbooks.com

Produced by PRC Publishing Limited,
The Chrysalis Building,
Bramley Road, London, W10 6SP, U.K.

An imprint of Chrysalis Books Group plc

All notations of errors or omissions should be addressed to Laurel Glen Publishing, Editorial Department, at the above address. All other correspondence (author inquiries, permissions, and rights) concerning the content of this book should be addressed to PRC Publishing Ltd, The Chrysalis Building, Bramley Road, London W10 6SP, U.K.

ISBN 1-59223-085-7

Library of Congress Cataloging-in-Publication Data available upon request.

Printed and bound in Malaysia

1 2 3 4 5 07 06 05 04 03

Acknowledgments

Jennifer Worick would like to thank the following lovely individuals for their assistance, knowledge, and support during the writing of this book: Sacha Adorno, Nancy Armstrong, Nicole Beland, Kerry Colburn, Margy Dooley, Josh Freely, Sylvia Gashi, Liesa Goins, Peter Gwin, Martha Lucy, Phyllis Richman, Laurel Rivers, Alison Rooney, Fil Scola, Caroline Tiger, Jared Von Arx, Melissa Wagner, and Ann Wilson. Thanks also to Martin Howard and Jo Messham for the opportunity.

PRC Publishing would like to thank Robyn Neild for supplying all the illustrations in this book, (© PRC Publishing Limited).

CONTENTS

Introduction

Welcome to the wonderful world of dating. Yes, dating can be exciting and even, dare I say, fun, if you are smart, prepared, and aware. Put bozos, putzes, cheapskates, jerks, and erstwhile dates from hell firmly behind you in your rear-view mirror as you sit in the driver's seat and head to the promised land.

But there's one thing you have to promise to do from the get-go. Namely, get yourself out there: outside, out of bounds, out of sight—just get yourself out of the house. And when venturing out into the world, you need to arm yourself with two things: a realization that you are being brave and this book.

Mr. Right is never going to knock on your door, unless he happens to be the mail carrier or the plumber, so you have to adjust your thinking. True love may not just show up when you think it's time; you have to put out a little effort to get any results.

You focus on your career, your workouts, and your finances. Why aren't you putting energy and time into crafting a satisfying social life? Carve out time in your daily, weekly, or monthly schedule to go out on the town or, more specifically, to meet potential dates. It doesn't have to be scary and you don't have to be alone while doing it. Go out with one or several friends. Go to the movies, your corner bar, or out to dinner. Resolve to be in the world.

Keep your eyes open at all times and be prepared to look in unconventional places: the gym, the line at the video store, the coffee shop you frequent, the pumps at the gas station, a crosswalk, the local swimming hole, a tour bus, a book-reading, a convention, a pet shop, an airplane, an airport—well, you get the idea. If this book is to benefit you in the least, you must commit yourself to opening up. You have to stop, look, listen, and then do the hardest thing: make eye contact, smile, or even say hello.

To figure out which milieu you are going to thrive in, take this short quiz and then I'll direct you to a chapter you might want to pay special attention to.

1 **Friday night of choice:**

- a Takeout and a movie on DVD ❐
- b Going to a movie with a friend ❐
- c Filming your own movie ❐
- d Sneaking onto the set of your favorite actor's new movie ❐

2 **First date of choice:**

- a Coffee shop on a Saturday morning ❐
- b Double date with your best friend ❐
- c Skydiving ❐
- d Drunken night carousing about town ❐

3 **Outfit of choice:**

- a Jeans and a sweater ❐
- b Swingy skirt or dress ❐
- c Leather pants ❐
- d Miniskirt, slinky top, or something equally revealing ❐

4 **Drink of choice:**

- a Herbal tea ❐
- b Glass of favorite Côte du Rhône ❐
- c The drink or happy hour special ❐
- d Mojito or drink de jour ❐

5 Music of choice:

a Jazz or R&B ❐
b Top-40 pop ❐
c Indie rock ❐
d Hip-hop ❐

6 Movie of choice:

a Weepy drama ❐
b Romantic comedy ❐
c Obscure independent or foreign film ❐
d Action-Adventure ❐

7 Exercise of choice:

a Yoga ❐
b Step class three times a week ❐
c Bike ride through a new neighborhood ❐
d Shaking your booty ❐

8 Meal of choice:

a Chicken breast prepared on Foreman grill ❐
b Pizza with mushrooms and pepperoni ❐
c Sushi ❐
d Steak frites ❐

9 Current home life of choice:

a Live alone with a cat ❐
b Have a place within a half an hour of parents' home ❐
c Share a house with a couple of roommates ❐
d Doesn't really matter, because you're never home ❐

10 Man of choice:

a Internet programmer who can recite the whole of *Star Trek 2: The Wrath of Khan* ❐
b Good listener who only speaks when he has something valuable to say ❐
c Starving artist with an impressive mental catalog of music ❐
d High-energy professional who knows all the bartenders in town ❐

If your answers were mostly As, you could be shy and/or enjoy solitary pursuits. Best to dip your toe into the dating pool by cruising men on Internet dating sites (see Chapter Three). You don't have to leave the house and you can be as private or open as you wish.

If you tended to pick B responses, you like safe environments, be it hanging out with friends or establishing a routine at the gym. I'd suggest making plans to go out often with your friends to new restaurants or favorite bars. You'll feel comfortable in the space and you'll be surrounded by people with whom you feel at ease. You may want to consider using a dating service. You can establish a level of trust and a relationship with one of the service's representatives. They do all the grunt work (picking out suitable men, making the dinner arrangements) and protect your privacy. The only thing you have to be nervous about is meeting your date.

If you picked several Cs, you have an artsy, experimental streak. You aren't afraid to try new things and you may get bored easily. Check out some of the edgier Internet sites (see Chapter Three), take a class, or place a personal ad (Chapter Four). With your adventurous spirit, you can be comfortable with any of the dating methods outlined in this book.

If you selected primarily Ds, my hat is off to you! You are brave and extremely social. You'd probably prefer to be out on the town than in on your sofa. Open yourself up to blind dates or speed dating (both in Chapter Four), and challenge yourself to visit different bars, restaurants, and clubs, even if you are flying solo (see Chapter Two).

Ready to have some fun? Let's go!

CHAPTER 1
Where to Begin?

So you've taken your first step and opened up this book. You can choose to read this in bed while plowing through a pint of ice cream and then just put it away after chuckling heartily over the witty writing. Or, better yet, challenge yourself to grow, go out into the world, and find someone or several someones with whom to share your ice cream.

Dating is often a puzzling endeavor and I'm going to do my best to demystify this ancient and seemingly barbaric ritual. First of all, figure out what you want out of the dating experience. Because you are reading this book, let's assume that you actually do want to date one or several persons. (This should not be taken for granted, as many of my friends and I have realized that at certain points in our single lives, we would rather be alone or hanging out with friends than out on a date. For me, my litmus test is if I'd rather be in a bubble bath reading a book than on a date with anyone—then I give myself permission to enjoy my singledom for a while.)

So think about what you would ideally like to get out of dating. Do you want to play the field, make a few male friends, seek out sexual partners, or hunt down Prince Charming? Do you want someone to go out with or someone to watch DVDs on the couch with?

If you are looking for one special man, then you need to figure out who you'd like this dreamboat to be. Taking a cue from the questions they ask you on dating websites when creating a profile, jot down some qualities you'd like your dreamboat to possess.

	Very important	Somewhat important	Doesn't really matter
Personality	❏	❏	❏
Sense of humor	❏	❏	❏
Looks	❏	❏	❏
Occupation	❏	❏	❏
Financially secure	❏	❏	❏
Where he lives	❏	❏	❏
Likes/has pets	❏	❏	❏
Athletic	❏	❏	❏
Education	❏	❏	❏
Religion	❏	❏	❏

Now that you know what's important and what's negligible/added bonus to you, sketch him out in your mind (check the blue boxes that follow):

First of all, what does he look like?

Hair

- Short ❏
- Long and scruffy ❏
- Bald ❏

Eyes

- Large and expressive ❏
- Cold and piercing ❏
- Too close together ❏

Height

- So tall you have to stand on tiptoes to kiss ☐
- Good things come in small packages ☐
- As long as he's taller than you, it's okay ☐

Weight/body type

- Muscular—you like to feel protected ☐
- Fit and toned ☐
- On the cuddly side ☐

Where does he live?

- City ☐ ☐
- Suburbs ☐ ☐
- Country ☐ ☐

What does he call home?

- House ☐ ☐
- Apartment ☐ ☐
- Historic building ☐ ☐
- Condo ☐ ☐
- Mobile home ☐ ☐
- The area over his parent's garage ☐ ☐
- His buddy's couch ☐ ☐
- His office ☐ ☐

What's his favorite thing to wear?

- His old college sweatshirt ☐ ☐
- A gold signet pinky ring ☐ ☐
- His grandfather's watch ☐ ☐
- A snappy fedora ☐ ☐
- A baseball cap ☐ ☐

What radio station is programmed on his stereo?

- Alternative station ☐ ☐
- NPR ☐ ☐
- Sports radio ☐ ☐
- College jazz station ☐ ☐
- Classic rock ☐ ☐
- He doesn't listen to the radio. He prefers books on tape. ☐ ☐

Does he read? If so, what?

- The newspaper ☐ ☐
- New nonfiction ☐ ☐
- Gothic or Victorian novels ☐ ☐
- Anything by Dr. Phil ☐ ☐
- A menu ☐ ☐
- *Maxim* ☐ ☐
- *New Yorker* (at least that's what he tells you) ☐ ☐

- Ads on the bus or subway ❑ ❑
- Research material for his dissertation ❑ ❑

What movies (or "films," as he likes to call them) will he drag you to see? ❑ ❑

- Action flicks ❑ ❑
- Tearjerkers ❑ ❑
- War dramas ❑ ❑
- Almodovar's newest film ❑ ❑
- Anything with Halle Berry ❑ ❑
- Witty indies where guys talk...a lot ❑ ❑
- Slasher movies ❑ ❑
- Teen comedies
- He won't drag you anywhere. He'll only watch movies on DVD. ❑ ❑

What kind of manners does he have? ❑ ❑

- Buses his own tables at cafés
- Holds open the restaurant door, but not the car door for you ❑ ❑ ❑ ❑
- Picks his nose furtively in public ❑ ❑
- Has been known to spit on occasion
- Let's the lady order first but would never order for her ❑ ❑
- Let's others cut in front of him at the cash register if they only have a few items ❑ ❑

- Will cut off his own mother in traffic ❑ ❑
- Bags his own groceries ❑ ❑

What quirks does he have?

- Can't live without his elaborate $5 coffee drink every morning ❑ ❑
- Has no sense of humor when you play with his childhood stuffed elf ❑ ❑
- Must watch HBO lineup on Sunday nights ❑ ❑
- Gets out of bed to double-check that he locked the door (which he did) ❑ ❑
- Loves to sing show tunes in the shower ❑ ❑

What's his favorite meal?

- Burger and fries ❑ ❑
- Mom's pot roast ❑ ❑
- The filet—rare—at the chichi French restaurant in town ❑ ❑
- Doesn't stop to eat ❑ ❑
- Sushi or interesting ethnic foods ❑ ❑
- Is allergic to garlic, legumes, onion, and shellfish and doesn't like asparagus, brussels sprouts, cucumber, olives, or melons of any kind. Oh yeah, scratch anything with squash in it. ❑ ❑

How does he feel about hygiene?

- Doesn't think to ever change his sheets ❐ ❐
- Doesn't have any sheets ❐ ❐
- Always tucks his shirt in, be it a T-shirt, turtleneck, dress shirt, polo shirt, etc. ❐ ❐
- Loves his hair product ❐ ❐
- Washes his hands religiously ❐ ❐
- Never lets his feet see the light of day ❐ ❐

Who does he hang out with?

- One of his many male or female friends ❐ ❐
- A few close buddies ❐ ❐
- He's a lone wolf ❐ ❐
- You, his future girlfriend ❐ ❐

What's his feeling about work?

- Lives to work ❐ ❐
- Works to live ❐ ❐
- Works for himself ❐ ❐
- Just biding his time until his around-the-world backpacking trip ❐ ❐
- In it for the money ❐ ❐
- Complains all the time but doesn't do anything about it ❐ ❐
- Job-hops with glee ❐ ❐

You get the idea. Now that you've figured out what you'd like in your man, try answering the same questions about yourself (check the pink boxes). Knowing what you want and who you are looking for is key but it's also essential to know thyself. Being more self-aware will help you to realize the vibe you are projecting into the world. In addition, you will be better able to figure out which places you will be most comfortable in and which will best showcase you and your personality. Lastly, you might come to recognize which parts of yourself you want to highlight and which you might need to do a little work on. Yeah, yeah, I know: You're perfect, just as you are.

* Insert Yourself into the World

If you don't already have a busy social life, join a club or group of some sort. Your alma mater probably has an alumni group in town. Some cities have social clubs for singles that host a variety of events, from hiking to playing billiards, each week. To find out if your city has such a group, check your local paper or do a search online. You can do something you enjoy or learn something new, as well as meet new people, some of whom will become your friends and invite you to parties and some of whom you may even choose to date.

I took a belly-dancing class with nineteen other women at a local college. It was a hoot and while I didn't meet any men, I became friendly with the instructor and a few people in class. I also had the opportunity to talk to men while parking my car and walking through the corridors of the college facility. I have remained in contact with a few friends I met there and now have a mean hip shimmy to unveil on a worthy date.

* A Friend in Need Is a Friend in Deed

Use your friends. Go out with them for coffee or a beer. Ask for their opinions on your outfit. See if they have any recommendations for places to search for boys. And yes, ask them if they know of any eligible men with whom you might hit it off.

But beware whom you ask. What your girlfriend thinks is an "eligible man" might not be exactly to your liking. Look at whom she tends to date. Does she fancy rich men who are more into being seen at the right restaurants in the right outfit than in having a good time? Does this make you cringe and want to hide out in your apartment in your decidedly unhip sweatpants?

Convey to your friends the type of man you are in the market for, as they may have a different guy in mind for you. You may think you'd like a guy in a rugby shirt who is working on his Ph.D., but your friends might think you'd be better off with a cultured older man who will treat you like a queen. Grab a few friends and a couple of bottles of wine and spend the evening drafting your dreamboat. You'll all be on the same page and ready to go to work for yourselves and each other.

I went on a press trip to a spa in Sedona, Arizona. It was breathtaking and relaxing and I was surrounded by women the entire time (if you don't count the three married resort executives who hosted us). I didn't know a soul when I arrived, but by the time I left, I had forged three solid friendships with amazing women. One of them, Sharon, had a vision during an emotional Reiki treatment. She saw me marrying her older, single, successful neighbor. Right on! Although the relationship has not materialized as of press time, this is the kind of chi I'm looking for in the world. I'm flinging myself out there on various adventures and the universe is telling me to keep hope alive. Okay, I realize I sound a bit New Agey; the energy of Sedona must have worked its magic on me.

Back to you. At this point, you've figured out who you're looking for and have a few ideas on how to engage yourself with the world and the people in it. So let's move on and demystify the oldest of meeting places—the bar.

A final note: I've assumed that this book is intended for single girls looking to date men. If in fact you are looking for a woman, forgive me and know that the same advice can apply when looking for a woman, as well.

CHAPTER 2
The Bar Scene

Love it or hate it, the bar is still a viable place to cruise for hotties. My friends constantly discuss the problem of where to meet eligible and desirable men. While television shows like *Sex and the City* make it seem like men are only a cigarette light away, it is a bit trickier in real life. If you love going out to crowded clubs, you will probably bump into men...literally. Opening your mouth and saying something clever or witty or sweet is another thing. Engaging a gent in conversation is one of the most powerful skills a single gal can possess. Obviously, you don't even get that opportunity if you are a homebody and hate the idea of the bar scene.

But there's hope for even the shyest, most sedate of you. The first trick to successful cruising is to pick a bar that suits you to a tee.

* The Food Chain of the Bar Scene

Just like drinks, music, food, and men, there is a bar for every taste. The trick is figuring out in which milieu you feel most comfortable. If you are at ease, you are going to project a more confident attitude that conveys that you are comfortable with yourself and approachable.

What type of establishment does your ideal man frequent? Is it a pub, a moneyed hotel bar, a dive? Maybe this mythical land of man doesn't exist. But you can happen upon a good guy every now and again if you are armed with information and are persistently social. Here are some of the more common drinking establishments:

The Pub

Usually Irish or English with a shepherd's pie or fish and chips on the menu, the pub is frequented by beer aficionados and dart enthusiasts. A pub is as close as you can get to a place where everyone—or at least the bartender and a few regulars—knows your name. While the first few forays into a pub might be a bit intimidating, especially if you are going it alone or a big sporting event is on TV, you will soon feel comfortable climbing onto a stool and ordering a Guinness.

From the outside, a pub might feature paned and/or bay windows and a painted wooden sign swinging in the wind. Common pub names include a combination of any or all of the following words: Owl, Thisle, Ye, Olde, Towne, Square, Peddler, Tam, Fiddle, Lad, Laddie, Gent, Yank, Shoppe, Shamrock, Shepherd, Pipes, Puss, Boots, Sixpence, Pirates of Penzance, Sullivan, McAnything, O'Anything.

Personality most suited to this bar: Lass next door

Drink of choice: Guinness

Typical guy: Former frat boy who loves his buddies and his beer. Usually wearing jeans and a sweater, this man does not stand on pretension and loves to gab.

Activity: Darts

Music: U2, The Cranberries, The Pogues

Vibe: Good-natured and friendly

Attire: Jeans and a snug cashmere sweater; light to little makeup.

Pick-up line: "What's good on tap here?"

The Dive Bar

The Dive Bar is a serious watering hole but can be a blast if you're in the right mood. If you get your second wind late in the evening, this fine establishment is just the ticket. The crowd can be either raucous or somnambulant, depending on the time of day or night and the number of patrons. But beware, just one bad apple can spoil the evening if he drinks too much and gets belligerent or violent. If you have a safe perch, however, this can be an entertaining spectacle to observe and then to discuss with the hottie wobbling on the stool next to you.

Personality most suited to this bar: Low maintenance and/or low budget

Drink of choice: A shot of Jack

Typical guy: Unshaven and perhaps sporting a ripe jean jacket, the man found at the dive bar may really enjoy drinking, to the point that he may have a problem. He might also like to drink on the cheap, because, well, he is cheap or financially limited.

Activity: Hard-core drinking, barfights

Music: Hank Williams, Rolling Stones, Lynyrd Skynyrd

Vibe: Beer-goggle-ly

Attire: Ripped jeans and an old concert T-shirt. You'll stick out like a sore thumb if you take too much care with your ensemble. Just throw something on and go.

Pick-up line: "Is it safe to order the hot dog?"

The Sports Bar

Woo hoo! While the crowd at the sports bar might resemble the pub, it is slightly different in flavor. The crowd may be younger and more blue-collar or collegiate in nature. These can often be found in the suburbs or in hotels, as well as college towns. If you are hankering for some hot wings or the latest on the baseball game, a sports bar is just the ticket. If there is a game on, however, beware. Do not attempt to talk to anyone while they are watching TV and do not get in their line of vision, unless it's halftime or the game is over. The crowd can be jubilant or angry or morose, but if you happen on the sports bar when the home team has won the game, don't be surprised if a man hugs or kisses you during the celebration. If you go on an off night, arm yourself with a few statistics and ask a cute guy about his rotisserie or fantasy baseball team or if he's got money on the upcoming game.

Look for sports metaphors to play a key role in the name of the sports bar: Players, Shooters, Team, Sports, Game, Fair Ball, End Zone, Halftime, Half Court, Full Court, Bullpen, Champions, Victors, Coin Toss, Penalty Box, Long Shot, Dunk, Hole in One, Seventh Inning Stretch, Home Run, Touchdown, First Down, Third and Long, Hatcheck, you get the idea.

Personality most suited to this bar: Tomboy

Drink of choice: Miller Genuine Draft or Budweiser

Typical guy: Sports fan, dude! This guy will probably be sporting a baseball cap so if you want a big head of hair on your man, find a way to get that hat off and check out his hairline. In addition, jeans, well-worn sneakers, and an old college sweatshirt or polo shirt would be right at home at the sports bar.

Activity: Watching TV, so avoid the sports bar when a big game is on unless you are a huge fan. You won't get anyone's attention, even if you're sporting serious cleavage.

Music: Bruce Springsteen, Bon Jovi, sundry musicians from New Jersey

Vibe: Jovial locker room or bleacher seat camaraderie.

Attire: Jeans and a sweatshirt from your alma mater or favorite team. If you own a baseball cap, this is the place to break it out.

Pick-up line: "What's the spread on the game?"

The Wine Bar

If your tastes in men, alcohol, and atmosphere run more toward the discriminating, a wine bar is a fabulous place to have a drink or two. The lighting is usually muted, the atmosphere is civilized, and the focus is on clever conversation and an impressive wine list. If you don't know your Chardonnay from your Cabernet, never fear. Ask a handsome man for some tips on navigating the wine list.

If the huge supply of wines on display doesn't give it away, the name of the bar may tip you off. It may actually have "wine" or "wine bar" in the name or include words like "grape," "harvest," "cluster," "label," or "vintage." The words will, however, be used in an elegant or tasteful way.

One of the features of the wine bar is the flight, where you can order several wines of the same varietal or in increasing body (start with a Beaujolais and end with a Zinfandel or Port, for example). If you spy an interesting-looking man and are feeling as bold as the house red, ask him if he'd like to share a flight. You may be sharing more than wine by the evening's end!

Personality most suited to this bar: Reserved sophisticate

Drink of choice: Your favorite varietal—please do not order, under any circumstances, White Zinfandel!

Typical guy: A well-groomed, cultured man, probably familiar with hair product. Could be slightly pompous but he'll give good conversation.

Activity: Perusing the wine list

Music: Smooth jazz, Edith Piaf, Norah Jones

Vibe: Classy and cultured

Attire: Long skirt, soft sweater, high boots or heels. Tactile fabric, such as velvet or silk, is in order here. Assault his senses!

Pick-up line: "Have you tried the Niebaum-Coppola Rubican?"

The Dance Club

A bit European with a touch of ghetto fabulousness, the dance club is a place to get down and get your groove on. If you are looking to shake your tail feather, this is the place to roost! It's dark and people are bumping and grinding—not the time to get suddenly bashful. Check your inhibitions at the door and dance suggestively toward someone you find sexy. Make and hold eye contact. Bust out your hottest dance moves and clothes. And remember to hydrate, for goodness sake! We don't want you fainting just when you're reeling him in.

Beware. Gay men love to dance and have rhythm, so you may be barking up the wrong tree if you set your sights on a well-groomed guy dancing on a riser to the sounds of Kylie Minogue.

Personality most suited to this bar: Bootylicious disco queen

Drink of choice: Water

Typical guy: The man who calls a disco home can often have a slick personality to accompany his slicked-back hair. He may be suave and throw money around freely in a bid for your attention. While he may be a nice man genuinely looking for love, it is prudent to tread with caution around this guy, even while you are dancing circles around him.

Activity: Voguing

Music: Techno, Madonna remixes, latest darling of MTV

Vibe: Crazy sexy cool

Attire: Skin is in. Slather on shimmer lotion and slip into a miniskirt and low-cut top. Since you are dancing, make sure nothing restricts your movement or your breathing.

Pick-up line: "Wanna dance?"

The Five-Star Hotel or Restaurant Bar

This is a rich man's hunting ground and you will most likely enjoy dark wood-paneled walls, soft lighting, and the smell of pricey cigars when you enter this men's club. However, you also get to be the center of attention amid the waves of testosterone. Slip up to the bar or sink into a comfortable leather club chair, languorously cross your legs, order up a serious cocktail, and take your pick of the well-bred litter.

Try this place out during the week during happy hour. You may be able to strike up a conversation with a gentleman looking to unwind after a stressful day of mergers and acquisitions. Who better to put him in a good mood than you, sister?

Personality most suited to this bar: Refined, with a head for business and a taste for the finer things in life

Drink of choice: Manhattan

Typical guy: A business executive in a perfectly tailored gray suit

Activity: Cigar smoking

Music: Old standards, courtesy of the piano bar

Vibe: Old money, power broker

Attire: Slip into a tailored suit and accessorize with elegant jewelry, quality shoes, and a serious handbag. Reveal something unexpected, such as a slit in a skirt or a halter top under your suit jacket.

Pick-up line: None. Wait for him to come to you.

The Hot Spot

This swanky club may have just opened and getting past the throngs at the front door is a triumph in itself. But your real victory awaits inside, as you sashay your way through the crowd that is hip to be cool. The club may have an exotic theme (Moroccan, African, Indonesian), complete with waterfalls, giant Buddhas, bindis on the waitstaff's foreheads, or belly dancers. Or it could be ultramodern and smooth, with harsh angles, cool lighting, floors that are lit from below, and images that are projected onto minimalist walls. Don't be surprised if you hear snippets of conversation referencing a new gallery opening or a private after-party.

Personality most suited to this bar: Downtown Diva

Drink of choice: Drink of the moment, be it a mojito, apple martini, or cosmopolitan

Typical guy: Player

Activity: Cruising

Music: Something smooth like Erykah Badu or something atmospheric that matches the theme of the club (Latin, moody, exotic, etc.)

Vibe: Think "P. Diddy private party" without the gift bag or the celebrities or the exclusive invitation

Attire: Trendy and "bling-bling." Trick out your designer-of-the-moment jeans or leather pants with lots of accessories. Add shimmery cream to your eyelids and cheeks to guarantee that you'll be mistaken for that certain hot new celebrity.

Pick-up line: "Is that Prada you're wearing?"

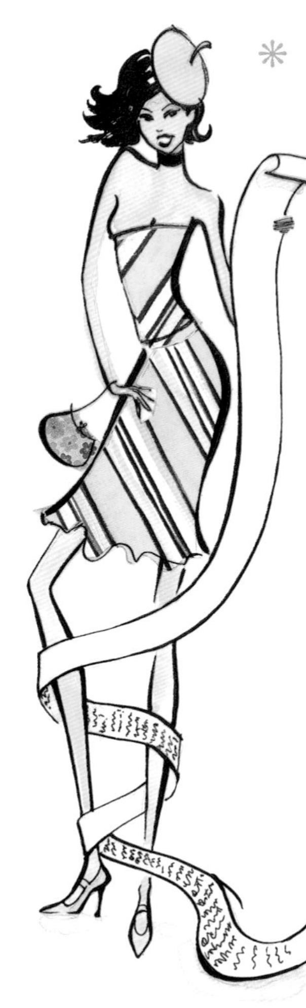

The Skinny on Pick-up Lines

It's nice to be yourself but sometimes it helps to have a bit of ammo in your arsenal. In other words, have an opening line at the ready should you bump into someone you like the look of. A sense of humor is always welcome but it's also nice to be sincere and ask something more substantial. Perhaps your flirting technique involves verbally abusing a boy (all in fun, of course) or you like to throw out outrageous opinions to spark his interest. Think about what has worked for you in the past in terms of what you were comfortable with and what men responded to, and go from there. Here are a few fun opening lines (albeit a bit cheesy) that never fail to get a response, even if they don't reel him in, hook, line, and sinker.

- Can I buy you a drink or do you want the money?
- The body is 90 percent water and I'm feeling quite thirsty.
- If I could rearrange the alphabet, I'd put U and I together.
- If I told you that you had a rock-hard body, would you hold it against me?
- Is it hot in here, or is it just you?
- Do you have any raisins? No, how about a date?
- I'm not feeling myself tonight. Can I feel you?
- Is that a mirror in your pants? I can see myself in them.

✻ Creative Methods of Meeting a Man

While it's nice to wait for a man to notice you, it doesn't always happen. Sometimes they need a little help. Aside from saying hello and introducing yourself, there are a few things you can do to make him sit up and take notice. Approach a guy and ask him to play along and pretend to know you. Tell him that someone (point out an unattractive person) is bothering you. Bump into him...literally. Buy him a drink; send it over with the bartender or waiter. Slip him a note on your way to the bathroom. Ask him for a light. Ask him for a cigarette. Ask him for the time.

Get it? If you don't have the gumption to spill a drink all over him, just think of something to ask him or talk to him about. It may seem hard to initiate contact at first but do it a few times and it'll become a piece of cake. If need be, practice on guys you aren't interested in before moving onto tastier men.

✻ Scoping Out Prospective Dates

First of all, I hope you have referred to the worksheet in Chapter One (see page 11) so you know just who you are looking for. Based on that information, use the bar profiles in this chapter to target places likely to house your kind of guy. And once you're in position, you can employ a few sneaky techniques straight from the pages of a Nancy Drew mystery to find out if you want to approach that tall drink of water leaning against the wall.

Note that none of these questions imply any sort of judgment and you should know that it's absolutely okay to have a thing against overly polished shoes or baseball caps worn backward. You like what you like so don't apologize. Just get busy looking for a guy who fits your general M.O.

Check out his appearance: Is he well-dressed? Do his clothes look shabby and worn, perhaps even stained and unclean? Does the man wear the clothes or is that purple suit wearing him? Is he sporting an expensive watch or a plastic digital thing he got out of a cereal box? Is that a man bag hanging from his right shoulder? Is he wearing shorts? Are his shoes shiny? Is he wearing Mardi Gras beads around his neck? Does the smell of weed linger about him? Does he know how to tie a tie properly? Is he wearing a wedding band or does he have a tan line where a ring ought to be?

What about his looks? Is he tall or short? Stocky or slender? Broad-shouldered? Does he have a flowing mane of hair or does he shave it so he's more aerodynamic? Are his knuckles particularly hairy, indicating a furry body beneath his clothes? Is his gaze mesmerizing or can't you tell because of a prominent Neanderthal brow ridge? Does he have an accent? Is his voice a deep bass or high pitched? Are those sideburns real? Does he have full lips? Do the corners of his mouth turn up in a grin all the time? Does he look, um, well-endowed?

Check out his demeanor: Is he with someone? Friends? A possible girlfriend? Is he friendly or chatty with the staff? Does he seem quiet and shy, taking in the scene but not engaging in it? Does his stare seem sexy or impertinent? Does he stalk around the room like a hungry jungle cat or does he keep his head down and avoid eye contact? Does he look as if he was born on that barstool and plans to die on it as well? Is he gabbing on his cell phone?

If you decide the pluses outweigh the minuses on your mental checklist, proceed to establishing contact, be it visually, verbally, or physically.

* Rose-Colored Glasses (i.e., Drunk)

I admit it. I've had beer goggles. I'm a lightweight so after about three beers, I think everyone looks pretty "do-able." After several unsavory experiences, I've learned to detect when my vision is becoming blurred and I'm becoming less than discriminating.

It helps if you have a friend to stick with when you're out and about. She can steer you toward men she thinks may be suitable for you and away from those who you think look just fine after several pints.

As you sashay out into the world, you want to be able to walk in a straight line (albeit seductively). Eat a meal before you go out and snack or eat while you are drinking. If you do start feeling tipsy, drink water immediately and get some fresh air. Stay on your feet. Avoid caffeine, as it will just make you a wired drunk. While feeling warm and fuzzy or bubbly and gregarious can be welcome emotions on the dating scene, the effects of drinking can also skew your ability to think and see straight and objectively.

Do:

- Drink plenty of fluids, especially water.
- Take a walk.
- Get fresh air.
- Vomit, if necessary—in private and over a toilet, if possible.

Don't:

- Drink coffee or other caffeinated beverages.
- Pass out on your back.
- Take over-the-counter pain-relievers, as they don't mix well with alcohol and can be dangerous.

* Hangover Remedies

These have all worked for someone but are not necessarily grounded in science. Eat what sounds good to you and listen to your body. You may need to try a few things before you figure out what works for you but that just gives you a reason to knock back a few more! After a vigorous night drinking my beloved cosmopolitan, a poppy seed bagel and a diet soda is my breakfast of champions.

- A large glass of water before bed
- Greasy food, be it an Egg McMuffin or a big diner breakfast with home fries
- Cold compress over eyes
- Ginger ale
- Chocolate milk
- Vitamin C

* Flirting

Some woman, damn them, are born flirts. Then there are those of us who need a bit of practice and a lot of help. Here are a few road-tested flirting techniques guaranteed to pique his interest. You may consider any or all of them beneath you but you probably have done any and all of these unconsciously at one time or another.

1. Bat your eyelashes and flip your hair. Winking and batting your eyelashes will draw his gaze to yours so you can exchange in some meaningful eye contact. Flipping or twisting your hair while you listen to him will indicate that you are engrossed in what he's saying.

2. Apply lipstick slowly. While it might seem rude to some, pulling out your creamy dreamy lip color and swiping some on without a mirror (or by looking into a spoon or knife) will focus his attention on your mouth and that is all good.

3. Lean in. Use your body to convey your interest. Lean in and rest your chin on a propped-up fist on the bar or table. Touch his forearm if he says something funny or you want to emphasize a point. He will get the message that you are bestowing yourself on him.

4. Giggle. Men love women who love to laugh (and they also like to think themselves funny). Let 'er rip.

5. Make eye contact. If you have a hard time holding his gaze for a long time, it's okay. Just smile and look away. Steal glances at him at regular intervals.

6. Give him hell. This is my favorite of the bunch. Find something about him about which to make a disparaging remark. For instance, question his manhood by his choice of an apple martini. But, never make a comment about his hairline! Make some gross assumption that you obviously would never know—"You've just gotten a big raise, haven't you? Buy me a drink?" You'll probably get a laugh and you will get his attention.

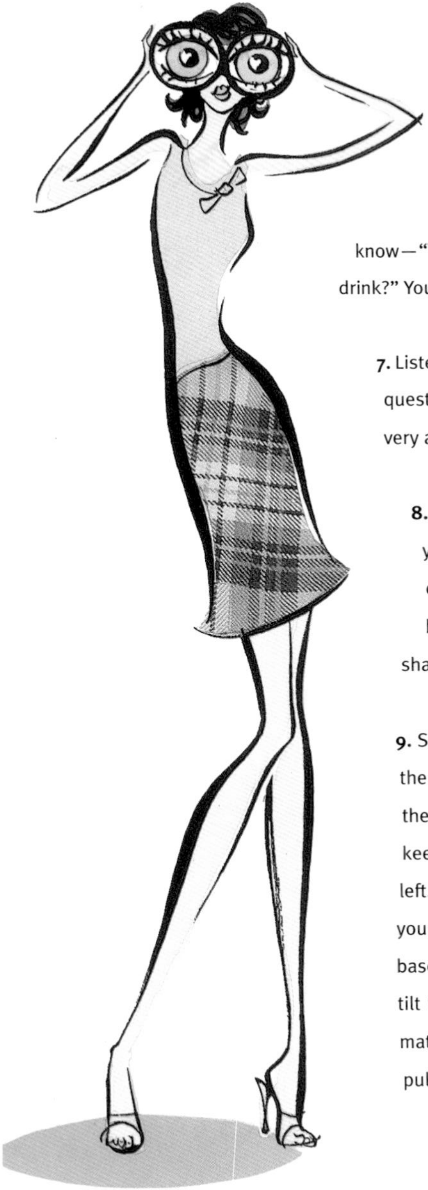

7. Listen to him. The best way to get to know him is to ask him questions and sit back and listen. Being a good listener is a very attractive quality.

8. Ask him for a light. If you smoke and he smokes, see if you can bum a cigarette or match. The smokers' community is strong and you can show your solidarity by sharing a cigarette (maybe you'll have a chance to share a ciggy later on...in bed).

9. Show him a trick or make a bet. Place a beer coaster on the table and a match on the table on the left-hand side of the coaster. Place a pint glass to the left of the match, and keeping part of the glass touching the table, tilt it to the left. While tilting it, push the coaster (and match) using your right hand under the glass until the match touches the base of the glass in the center. Holding the coaster in place, tilt the glass back and forth until it balances against the match without holding it (this takes some practice.) Then pull the coaster away with your right hand and wave it under the pint glass, which seems to be balancing all on its own. You appear to be magical!

10. Get his digits. Get his number rather than giving yours out. Unless you know this guy through friends or otherwise know him to be trustworthy, only dole out your cell phone number or an e-mail address that won't reveal your real name. If you feel bold, hand him a matchbook, coaster, or napkin with your number on it. If you've been talking shop and know he's on the level, slip him your business card. To really jerk his chain, grab a permanent marker and write it on his hand. This is a good one because if he freaks out, he probably has a girlfriend who won't understand why he has your number on his palm.

* Make Friends in High and Low Places

After trying on a few bars for size and finding one that fits your personality, make it your own. Frequent it with friends or even alone. Learn the layout of the joint. Make a point to chat up the bartenders and waitstaff. They can prove valuable allies throughout your dating experience. Dating can be exhausting and if you know the supporting characters in your drama, it makes it that much easier to relax and focus on the guy across the table or on the stool next to you. And duh, palling around with the bartender is guaranteed to score you free drinks on more than one occasion.

It's a snap to make the bartender your buddy. Treating him like a person rather than a drink dispenser is a good start. If there's a slow period, ask him for a good horror story of a drunk, cheap, or bitchy customer. Ask him what his specialty is or what the best drink on the menu is. Describe what kind of drink you like and ask for his opinion on another you might fancy. If it's crowded, make a joke along with eye contact. He'll be more likely to remember you the next time you hop on a barstool during his shift. Above all, be courteous, tip generously, and patronize the same place with some frequency.

CHAPTER 3
The Skinny on Internet Dating

It used to be a bit of a punch line. “My sister married some guy she met on the INTERNET!” But Internet dating has not only shed its stigma, it has become a legitimate way to get to know and like people, to develop relationships that last longer than one excruciating cup of coffee in a well-lit, populated place.

And heck, it’s a blast! As someone who has dated quite a few men who I met online, I can say that you can be smart and targeted in your search and meet some terrific people. Whether you are looking for lasting love or just a riotous social life, Internet dating sites are just the ticket. However, you need to be savvy in order to have a fulfilling experience. You can go back and tweak your profile, you can look as much or as little as you want at other ads, and you can freeze and reactivate your account as you have time.

But where do you start? Obviously, people are busy. And navigating various websites, creating profiles, and cruising ads takes time and can be a bit complicated. But you aren’t learning a foreign language. You are just trying to expand your social circle. Hard, yes. Rocket science, nope. So let’s get you plugged in—I’ll take you through selecting a site, creating a profile, surfing other people’s ads, e-mailing in a safe and fun environment, and taking the relationship offline and out on the town.

Is Internet Dating for You?

The most common argument heard against online dating is that you can't really tell what the person is like and if you have chemistry. The guy you've been corresponding with for two weeks who says he's an investment banker who does carpentry on the weekends and looks like a young Harrison Ford in his online photo could, in actuality, be a short-order cook who collects Pez and looks more like Chewbacca than Han Solo. Not that there's anything wrong with that, but he may not be who you signed on for.

Internet dating can be a crapshoot but at least you are in the game. And it certainly isn't any more random than meeting someone in a bar. In fact, you can prescreen and deep-six anyone and everyone who looks suspicious, dirty, uninteresting, cheesy, poor, rich, ugly, handsome, you name it. And while a prospective man may be trying to reel you in with a few well-placed mistruths, you can also use the medium to reinvent yourself. You can be the mystery woman you've always longed to be or you can be innocent and sweet.

Selecting the Right Website

More and more dating sites are cropping up for every age, religious/ethnic background, and personality. It pays to use a good search engine to ferret them out and to spend some serious time just cruising various sites before committing to one or a few. Check out the site's ease of use, success stories, rates, and policies, particularly its security measures.

I'd also recommend keeping your eyes open for unconventional ways to connect via the Internet. Both dating services and personal ads are offered on many career/professional websites, and many sites abound for different religious persuasions and so forth. There's something for everyone and new sites crop up daily.

That said, several dating websites have been around for a few years and have an established track record. Here are a few to check out:

Match.com: This is the granddaddy of the dating websites. Boasting four million profiles, there's certainly someone here for you, if only for a fun chat or first date. It's free to join and search profiles but there is a modest monthly fee for sending e-mail. The site is very easy to navigate and it walks you through setting up a profile.

Metrodate.com: This site features a sizable clientele, it's easy to navigate, and security measures are terrific. It's free to post a profile (with up to three photos) and receive messages from interested parties, but you must purchase tokens or a monthly package if you wish to initiate contact and send someone a message. You can narrow your search by a variety of criteria, including geographic proximity, religion, age, race, height, and compatibility with your own questionnaire.

Matchmaker.com: Another popular dating site, matchmaker.com asks members to complete a lengthy essay in addition to a thorough questionnaire. You can do some cursory searches and eliminate potential suitors by photo alone (let's face it—looks do matter). A recording option lets you check out his voice. The first week is free; after that, you pay a monthly fee.

Nerve.com: For an edgier, alternative crowd. The site asks more interesting, thoughtful questions so your profile doesn't end up sounding like a cliché ad. However, this is a double-edged sword. I checked out one man's profile I liked until I got to the end of his list of the top ten reasons to date him. The number-one reason? He has great-tasting, um, you know. I don't know whom he thinks he's going to reel in with that bit of information but it wasn't going to be *me*. Lesson learned? Read the entire profile, don't just chuckle at his opening sentence and skim the rest. A profile is rife with details and clues.

Hypermatch.com: This site's 400-question survey may scare off all but the most intrepid of daters, but get this: Based on your answers, this free site will perform some mathematical magic and match you up with compatible users.

Greatboyfriends.com: This juicy little site features men who have been recommended by previous girlfriends, sisters, or female pals. For twenty bucks a month, you can be assured of a guy's quality. However, the women on the site far outrank the men so you may have to wait. If you know of any good guys out there who aren't for you, nominate them for the site and do the rest of us a favor!

Flirt.com: Designed for perky, younger singles, this website lets you post a free profile, but there's a monthly fee for sending and receiving e-mails. This site isn't focused on making a long-term love connection as other sites, but if you want to flirt, make this your cyber destination.

Lavalife.com: Whatever your pleasure, this site has it. For a small fee, you can search this site by dating, relationships, or intimate encounters.

Yahoo Personals: The personals section of yahoo.com has a large database of entries. It figures out how good a match you are with the people listed and gives you a percentage figure of how potentially compatible you are.

Chat rooms: Don't forget about chatting up guys in all the nooks and crannies of the Internet. While not as popular as when the Web first took off, chat rooms are still viable ways to connect with people who share similar interests, hobbies, political views, or careers. If you want to meet someone in your line of work or who is passionate about a particular television show or environmental issue, then check out a chat room.

* Creating Your Profile

Now that you've zeroed in on an Internet dating site, it's time for the moment of truth. Cue music. Okay, it's not that dramatic. In fact, creating a profile can be a ton of fun. After all, how often in life do you have the opportunity to reinvent yourself? Pretend this is the first day at a new high school and you are the mysterious cat's meow.

Advertising yourself may seem a bit crass or unseemly but think of it this way: When you go on a first date, you take care to look good. You swig some mouthwash, avoid clothes with visible stains, and remember to not pick your teeth during dinner. You are constantly working hard to make a good impression. Well, you don't have the chance to do that in person; your web profile is all you've got to work with. You know you're a catch but you've only got a couple of seconds to catch someone's eye. So how do you spark someone's interest long enough to review your profile and then go to the next level of e-mailing you?

Your Message

The biggest and probably most important part of your profile is the written description of yourself and your ideal mate. Before you do anything else, establish who you are looking for. Is a prime physical specimen of utmost importance? Does he need to be loaded, kind, kinky, or above all else, have a sick sense of humor? Thinking about the person you are ultimately looking for and what qualities are important for him to have will help you to market yourself effectively.

Next, what are your best qualities? Enlist the help of your friends, who probably see you differently than you see yourself. You might think yourself shy, but a friend might say that you're a great listener. Friends can also help you emphasize your best physical traits. You may not like your smile, but a pal might say you light up a room when you giggle. Many of us have the tendency to be modest, even in our own heads. Now is not the time to hide your light under a bushel!

Brainstorm without putting limitations on yourself. When you've exhausted the possibilities, go back and highlight the qualities, traits, or skills that match your dream mate. For instance, if you are looking for a hottie that loves eighties music, you might want to emphasize that you work out five times a week and only a mix of Bon Jovi and Duran Duran can make you sweat. Fancy a type-A workaholic or yoga instructor? Write it down! Specifics are terrific, as they act as kind of a private joke that someone out there will love to get.

Profiles include dislikes and turnoffs, as well as the good, positive stuff. Be honest! If you are tired of your clothes smelling like smoke after every date, eliminate smokers. Poof, they're gone. Need your other to possess a certain income level to court you in the style to which you've become accustomed? Ch-ching. Just say the word. Looking for a dog lover? Grrr, giddyup. The great thing is that you can ask for anything and anyone you want. You may not get many responses right away, but the e-mails that you do get may be right on.

On the flip side, what bad habits are you willing to live with and what must be kicked to the curb? What did you like or dislike about past relationships? You may have blocked the image of your ex-honey's affinity for filth but now is the time to remember it in vivid detail. Rather than stating it as a negative, admit that you're looking for someone who loves the smell of Murphy's Oil Soap and isn't afraid to use it.

Now that you've got the critical information figured out—who you are and who you're looking for—have some fun. Include some unique, quirky, or downright bizarre information that is sure to grab some attention. Are you addicted to

Trading Spaces? Were you once the Donkey Kong world champion? During your teenage years, did you work on an assembly line, screwing shut tubes of mascara? Are you double-jointed? Can you recite the dialogue from *Deliverance*, twang and all? When meeting David Duchovny, did you resemble Cindy Brady in front of the red light and fail to say a single coherent word?

When I first posted a profile, I was a bit overwhelmed by the e-mails I received from men savvy enough to realize I was a catch. I ended up e-mailing only one guy, because he threw in a reference to dating Marcia in order to steal Greg's playbook. Genius! How could he have known that the *Brady Bunch* is my favorite TV show of all-time?! I was sure we were soul mates.

Again, think about something special about yourself that might appeal to the kind of person you're looking for. If intelligence is key, add an obscure reference to your ad. If you're looking for a laugh riot, include a fun pop culture reference that reveals your goofy side. If you want a kind-hearted sports fanatic, sneak in a detail about how you cried when the Red Wings won the Stanley Cup.

Here's one of the messages I have posted on a website:

> Let's see. Hmm, where should I start? I'm a freelance writer who has the good fortune to write sassy books and articles. The highlight of recent months was raiding the beauty closet at *Cosmo* magazine (I have friends in high places). My beauty booty was the envy of all my friends, but lucky for them I spread the wealth (and green mascara doesn't suit me anyway).
>
> I love all sorts of pop culture and believe *Die Hard* to be the best action film ever made. It's in my top five, along with *Sunset Boulevard*

and other black-and-white movies with snappy dialogue and men in hats. I love sushi and Thai food. I have an impressive collection of Nancy Drew mysteries and Betty and Veronica comic books (Archie was dreamy). I try to get out as much as possible, seeing as working at home is distracting, what with cable TV and my pile of unread books and magazines. I enjoy knitting and belly dancing, my toes are always polished, and I can recite a longish passage from *The Godfather.* I am thirty-two flavors and then some, and I think I've detailed about four and a half here. That's enough to get you started, methinks. Oh yeah, my favorite ice cream flavor these days is that new caramel extravaganza from Ben & Jerry.

Even though I am pretty great, I'm not looking for someone just like me. I generally like men who dig pop culture, like boy things like March Madness and PS2, have their favorite hole-in-the-wall restaurant or bar, are kind to waitstaff, aren't allergic to cats or strawberries, and like to laugh a lot.

The Questionnaire

The next part of the profile usually includes a yes/no or multiple-choice questionnaire that asks for your preferences as well as for personal information you may not have included in your written description.

Again, this is an excellent opportunity to further define the kind of person you are looking for. city vs. suburbs, indie rock vs. classical music, adventurer vs. homebody, tattoos vs. piercings, blond vs. brunette. You can be shallow without guilt, as you are just answering questions the site is asking you! Avail yourself of the chance to separate the wheat from the chaff. You know what to include, but you should carefully evaluate what information it might be better to keep to yourself for the time being. Do not answer anything you are uncomfortable with. For instance, some sites ask for your income level. Both men and women are usually reluctant to tell even their friends and family what they are pulling down annually. Be thoughtful when deciding whether to answer this question. You also might be skittish describing the condition of your body. Sites often ask multiple-choice questions on such topics, and it's tricky to decide whether to sell yourself up or be more modest.

The Headline

After you've completed the questionnaire and written a paragraph or two about yourself and who you're looking for, review this information and note the general feel of the profile. Is it breezy or tongue-in-cheek? Is it earnest and sincere? Is it playful? Seductive? Once you get a flavor, draft a headline for your profile. Most sites ask that you do this first but I think it's helpful to get the other information down first. Then you can title your ad. Again, think of how you can reflect the spirit of the profile while distinguishing yourself from the pack. Ballsy claims, a self-effacing comment, references to pop culture or obscure trivia, a phrase that has nothing to do with your ad and is solely intended to catch someone's eye—all of these headlines can prove wildly effective.

I thought I'd strike an ironic note with a headline that poked fun at the whole personals gig. "Doesn't everyone like a walk on the beach?" was meant to be tongue in cheek but too many guys thought I was a beach bunny. The great thing about a profile is that you can change or tweak it at any time. My profile later sported a reference to the greatest writer in the history of mankind: Dr. Seuss.

The Photograph

Do photographs really matter? People have certainly found each other on sites and in chat rooms without the benefit of a photograph. However, barring an abnormally large goiter, you are more likely to receive responses to your profile if you have a photo in place. Get a load of this statistic: Profiles with photos are cruised eight times more often than those without. If you don't post a picture, it probably won't be long before someone with whom you're e-mailing asks for a visual. And be honest, you are more likely to e-mail someone if you dig on his profile *and* photo.

Aside from good versus questionable looks, you can tell quite a bit about someone from his picture. Surroundings, clothing, and expression are all on display, so take care to make sure the photo you post matches the image you want to convey.

I e-mailed one young man because he was sitting in a massive purple chair that resembled a throne. Most of my e-mail was grilling him on why he was perched in such a splendiferous seat. His surroundings reeled me in and then provided an entrance for a fun conversation. Needless to say, he fell off his chair he was so charmed by me!

It's a snap to post a photo if you have a digital camera or scanner. Just create an electronic file of your photo (jpg, eps, or tiff files are usually acceptable) and e-mail it to the website as an attachment. The site will include guidelines and an e-mail address for sending photos. A few sites will allow you to send actual photographs to them but it will take a bit longer for the photo to be placed with your profile.

As far as what photo to post, choose your favorite or most flattering. Ideally, you should be smiling or at least look happy. You can use a headshot or a full-body photo, or you can include both if the website allows multiple photos. If there are others in the photo, make sure they are cropped out. Try to select a photo where the background isn't too busy. If you have a photo that shows you doing something you love, be it bungee jumping or playing barista with your espresso machine, by all means include that. It gives users a sense of your flavor and personality.

So at this point, you've got a headline, a description of who you are and who you are looking for, a questionnaire that has narrowed the playing field to only serious contenders, and a decent photo that reveals the essence of your true being. I think you're ready to go live with your profile and prowl some ads yourself. Let the games begin!

* Looking for Mr. Right

Surfing profiles of potential dates is one of the most enjoyable activities in life. You get to be the proverbial kid in a candy store and there's no nasty toothache after you binge. You can usually wade through dozens or even hundreds of profiles with discretion and ease. Once you've completed your own questionnaire, you can have the site match you up with other like-minded users. Matches can range from five to fifty people, depending on the site and how specific you are choosing to be. You can cast a wide net and then narrow it down, or start with a very focused group and then see how the pool changes as you alter the search criteria. Or you can just look at profiles of men in your geographic region and spend a very satisfying evening or weekend plowing through this "raw data."

Regardless of how many profiles you have to peruse, there are a few ways you can make the most of your time. In a word, skim. Look at the photos and if one catches your eye, check out the guy's stats, his ability to string together sentences or thoughts, and his voice (if that option is available). Or you can choose to skim by age, weight, religious convictions, income, eye color, vacation preferences (really), or whatever trait or quality is important to you. Again, you are doing this privately so you can narrow your search however you choose.

In reading his profile, take note of a few key words that might be euphemisms for less-attractive qualities, or red flags to more serious issues (see page 46 for a few examples). Of course, he may be great and exactly as he describes himself, but if you get a bad impression from his profile or he tries to push one point too much, you may want to keep looking.

He says he:	He may mean that he is actually:
Likes strong women	Lying or wussy
Has a great sense of humor	Laughing at his own jokes
Is sensitive	In possession of a fragile ego
Loves walks on the beach	Unoriginal
Thirty-five and never been in a long-term relationship	Emotionally unavailable
Looking for his best friend	Needy
Is a workaholic	Controlling
Spends weekends working on his house	Insulated, materialistic
Has lots of friends	Not good at intimacy
Loves films by David Fincher and Todd Solondz	Scary
Likes a woman who knows what she wants	Passive
Likes fast cars and fast women	Looking for one-night stand
Works out every day	Vain

✳ Crafting your First E-mail

So you've found someone potentially worthy of you and you are ready to make contact. There are a lot of approaches you can take when e-mailing a guy for the first time. I like to pick out something from his message or photo that catches my eye. If he makes a vague reference to a book you recently read, ask him how he felt about a particular plot point. If he is pictured with a chocolate lab, ask what her name is and mention that she's the spitting image of your childhood pet, Mona.

There's no rule about length but in my experience, you are more likely to get results if you personalize the message and make it longer than just one or two sentences, with the request to "check out your profile." If you don't put time into the communication, why should he? This is your chance to make a good first impression and intrigue him. Don't waste the opportunity!

Ask him questions. Questions invite answers (i.e., he'll be more likely to write back and you've given him a place to start), and if you express interest in him, he'll feel like an interesting, valued person. Stroke that ego, baby! You can ask about stuff from his profile, about current events, movies, or music, or you can ask him his position on the spate of tapas bars opening up around town. Ask him whatever you want but keep it light. This is not the time or place to ask him about politics, therapy, or past relationships. That's what the first date is for! (Just kidding.) If you think you'd like to weed out suitors pretty quickly with a thorough line of questioning, be prepared to send the faint of heart running for cover.

Tell him a few choice details about yourself but mix it up. Don't simply repeat information from your profile; he'll get to that pretty quickly after your e-mail if he's interested. If you have been taking yoga lessons and say so on your profile, casually mention that you're excited about an upcoming retreat that you will be attending soon. If you just discovered a new Belgian beer, clue him in so he can wow his friends next time he's at the pub.

Be true to yourself in your e-mail. Don't strike a tone that you think will please him but is unnatural for you, be it funny, sexy, or deeply earnest. Don't pretend to be someone you're not, unless you are looking to have a fun, maybe temporary encounter. This is an opportunity to reinvent yourself but take care not to get so carried away with your new persona that it becomes a game rather than a chance to make a meaningful connection.

* In the Thick of It

Once you've set up your profile, be prepared for a barrage of e-mail. Initially, longtime users will see your profile or photo and jump at the opportunity to meet someone new. Depending on the site and the number of users, you could receive a dozen e-mails in your first week. If you can, read all of them. If you like what you read, move on and check out the profile. If you still are intrigued, go ahead and respond. Maintain your privacy and use the site's messaging service as long as you feel unsure of the person. He may ask for your personal e-mail, since it may cost him each time he messages you. Do not give it out, unless you have a separate e-mail account that does not give away your real name or personal information (many e-mail services allow you to create multiple names and addresses for free).

When filtering out potential suitors, I admit I am persnickety. If they use horrible grammar, can't spell, write in all caps, or use way too many ellipses, I may give them the boot. If the content of their message is dull, then out they go. I value myself and just like when I'm out in the real world, I use filters and instinct to narrow the playing field.

Once you've received numerous responses, how many men can you feasibly juggle electronically? Well, I find that I can only comfortably communicate with three guys simultaneously. More than that and I forget to whom I said what and I confuse their personalities and profiles. Tip: Save all of your messages so that if memory fails you, you can reconstruct an electronic conversation. You may find that you can only focus on one at a time or perhaps you are having a ball chatting up five or six boys in one evening. See how it goes and find a number that works for you.

Also, if you are having fun with six men, figure you are going to wind up on six dates if all goes well. That may be just what you're looking for but if you want a serious relationship, you may find that you have to dismiss men one by one until you find your favorite. And that can be a bit messy.

I think it's fine to e-mail as often as you want. Respond to his e-mail as quickly or slowly as you see fit. You may find yourself in a late night tête-à-tête that resembles an instant messaging tennis match. Go with it. Have fun—after all, isn't that why you're doing this?

✳ Taking It Offline

So you've been e-mailing for a couple of weeks and digging it. What do you do now? Take it to the phone, preferably cell phone (for safety reasons—he can't track down your address) if you've got the free minutes. I strongly recommend not waiting too long before talking on the phone or meeting your man. You get to know someone in a certain way via e-mail and you have to discover him anew when you meet him in person. The chemistry and ease of conversation can be completely different. I went on a date with a guy I thought was perfect after a torrent of hilarious e-mails. Well, he thought I was perfect, too, and told me so. Frankly, it creeped me out. He felt we had already established a relationship and level of intimacy on e-mail, so he felt fine moving in for the kill, so to speak, on the first date. What he managed to kill was any positive feeling I had for him and I had to break it off quickly. So heed my tragic cautionary tale—don't get too involved in your e-mail relationship before actually meeting in person.

Back to the phone. You can pick up a few clues on the telephone, such as confidence, deepness of voice, intelligence, etc. Again, you are kind of chatting anonymously, so let your jitters go and have fun. Take care not to get too sexy in your conversation; it may send him the wrong message if you are more interested in a long-term relationship than getting jiggy wit it. And it's really easy to let your guard down on the phone and make suggestive comments or whisper things in a husky voice. If you wouldn't say something to his face, don't say it into his ear!

Contact!

So you've gotten as far as setting up a meeting. Congratulations! You've found someone interesting enough to meet. This calls for a drink. I highly recommend setting up a meeting at a café or bar for a drink. That way, the first date is kept to an hour or so. You have the option to continue the date, leave him wanting more, or leave him with the image of you walking out the door. I'd also recommend meeting at a place you're familiar with. You'll be more at ease and know all the escape routes. And if you know the waitstaff and bartenders, they can keep an eye out for you!

Chapter Four will give you a host of suggestions for discussion topics and conversation starters if you find yourself tongue-tied and staring into your glass. See Chapter Five for more tips on staying safe, looking great, and following up after the first date.

* Freezing your Account

In the world of cyber dating, agreeing to freeze your respective accounts is akin to going steady. You are agreeing to concentrate on each other and see where the relationship goes. Of course, each of you could have a profile on another site or under another name (hopefully with no photos) but just like any relationship that continues to progress, you are deciding to trust each other and date exclusively.

So even though it's a breeze to freeze and reactivate your account, make sure this is the message you want to send your beau. If you, on your own, decide to freeze your account because you're suddenly really busy and unable to field e-mails from numerous men, you may want to think twice. Your guy might get freaked thinking that you consider yourself going steady with him. Conversely, he may be ready to take it to the next level and this will confirm that you think the same. Mention your reasons for freezing the account, so he doesn't get the wrong idea. Sometimes men surprise you and read into things!

MOT RS
MECH ANICS
SOCCER
FLY FISHIN
GARDENING

✻ The Skinny on Sophie

Let me leave you with a success story. My friend Sophie has been doing the Internet dating thing for nigh on a year now. Before venturing into the waters of Internet dating, Sophie had been a big girl who dated very little. She had never had a long-term relationship and she was well into her thirties. With the assistance of a doctor, nutritionist, and fitness instructor, Sophie went on a liquid diet and lost eighty pounds.

Looking fantastic and armed with a healthy attitude after years of being judged on her appearance, she dated thirteen men in the course of a year. She dated one man for five months. They even traveled to Hong Kong. But he broke it off with her because her weight was an issue for him. Nice of him to figure that out after months and months!

Anyway, after Marcello, Mike, Steve, Stephen, Mark, Ken, John, Kurt, Tyler, William, Scott, Mike, and Michael, Sophie found Bert. After two weeks of dating, they froze their accounts to concentrate on each other. I think what sealed the deal is that after a few dates, Bert fessed up to the fact that he had recently lost forty pounds. I hope they are meant to be, and at this point all signs point to yes! But this wasn't divine intervention. Sophie stuck with it and kept looking and e-mailing and talking and dating and starting all over again. So stick with it; you may very well find your own Bert someday.

If you decide that you want to look for your own Bert elsewhere, just freeze your Internet account. It usually takes less than five minutes and you can reactivate it at any time. I froze my account and went underground for a couple of years while I dabbled in more traditional forms of dating. But I recently went back to the Internet and reactivated my account. Not only was my profile still intact, all the messages I had received and sent were still archived for my viewing pleasure. It was kind of fun to check out these guys, but also it was helpful to see the person I was back then. She was pretty cool, if I do say so myself.

CHAPTER 4
Dating Services, Personal Ads, and Speed Dating, Oh My!

There are several ways for the intrepid single woman to meet men. If you want to take the bull by the horns, this chapter is for you. In the expanding singles culture, new methods of meeting men are constantly cropping up and old traditions are being refined and updated. Dating services are making it easy for busy professionals to meet in low-pressure environments. One service even matches you up with compatible millionaires! Speed-dating services allow you to cycle through available men every few minutes and decide at evening's end who you want to see for a longer stretch of time. Matchmaker services and social coaches are sprouting up to assist saucy singles in their quest for a full dance card. But which one is for you?

* Dating Services

After some initial consultations and questionnaires, dating services do much of the grunt work for you in finding compatible men. You may be asked to supply a photo or the service will take one for you. A few even videotape a short interview with you for screening by possible dates. However, the expense can be considerable (upward of $1,000 in some cases) and the choice is taken out of your hands. But if you want to guarantee dates with eligible men that fit your criteria, this is a good method.

Millionaire's Club

This dating service features a male clientele who are all millionaires. It is free for women to join and you can get an application from the service's website (millionairesclub123.com). In addition to the form, you must supply one or several professional studio photos (submitting head shots and full-length photos are recommended). Note, however, that the site is looking for well-groomed and well-bred women of a particular age range. The service will review your application and call you for an appointment if there is a millionaire it feels is a good match.

It's Just Lunch

In business for more than ten years, It's Just Lunch! is a dating service marketing itself to busy professionals. After a confidential interview, the service determines what you are looking for in a potential partner and what qualities are most important to you.

At that point, a customer representative reviews its male client database and pulls any potential matches. She then arranges a lunch, brunch, or drink date for you and your match. She even makes the reservation! The idea is that It's Just Lunch is setting up a short and sweet first date so that you can relax and enjoy the date (or know that it'll be over in an hour!). However, the cost is considerable—fees can run as high as $1,600 for twelve dates.

A woman I know used this service and was generally happy with the results. Susan had requested a professional with a graduate school level of education. In one case, the service hooked her up with a man who owned his own business but on the date, Susan found out that the man had not even graduated from high school. She contacted the service to complain and they did not count this date as one of her twelve. It pays to speak up if they set you up with someone who clearly doesn't match your profile. In another instance, Susan met a man at a popular bar for drinks after work only to discover halfway through the date that the woman at the next table was laughing and flirting with the guy Susan was supposed to meet. The service had set up two dates at the same bar at the same time and a date swap had accidently occurred. She and her date laughed about it but it looked like the other couple was really getting along. Susan wishes them the best.

* Personal Ads

Personal ads have long been a mainstay of the singles world. Al Pacino explored their more dangerous side in *Sea of Love*. Hope Davis revealed the ridiculousness of it all in *Next Stop, Wonderland*. And, well, personals can be a bit of both. Now that Internet dating sites have grown by leaps and bounds, personal ads have taken on a slightly seedier reputation. The perception is that personal ads are geared toward more adventurous folks looking for a one-time sexcapade. These ads can certainly be found amid the requests of a DWM looking for a threesome, but there are men genuinely looking to make a love connection.

First things first. Look through various publications and find one you are comfortable with and whose ads match your dating desires. If there is an ad that catches your eye, call a voice mailbox and leave your guy a message. If he calls you back, I strongly recommend having a few conversations over the phone to get to know each other before meeting for coffee or a drink.

If you are feeling brave, draft a message, call the paper, and read your ad over the phone. The cost of the ad depends on how many words or lines it is but it's usually very affordable (rates are higher for papers or magazines with larger circulations). The publication will run the ad and set you up with a mailbox where interested parties can record messages for you. You can then take your pick of the litter and call them back as you wish.

Personals: A Primer

What the heck do all those letters mean? Here is a guide to the most frequently used abbreviations.

A: Asian

B: Black

BI: Bisexual

C: Christian

D: Divorced

DDF: Drug/Disease Free

F: Female

FTA: Fun Travel Adventure

G: Gay

H: Hispanic

ISO: In Search Of

J: Jewish

LD: Light Drinker

LDS: Latter Day Saints

LS: Light Smoker

LTR: Long-Term Relationship

M: Male

MM: Marriage Minded

NA: Native American

NBM: Never Been Married

ND: Non Drinker

NS: Non Smoker

P: Professional

PR: Puerto Rican

S: Single

SD: Social Drinker

SI: Similar Interests

SOH: Sense of Humor

W: White

Wi: Widowed

YO: Years Old

Drafting your Ad

Much of the advice for creating your profile for an Internet site (see Chapter Three) applies here, except for one thing. You need to be brief and concise. So what should you write?

If you are interested in a relationship, steer clear of sexy talk. In a short message, anything that sounds more sexy than sassy will convey the wrong idea. Describe yourself with a few abbreviations; since you aren't providing a photo, you need to give something for readers to visualize. Think about your best traits and reel them off—witty, great cook, film junkie. Think back to the main qualities you are looking for and detail a few of those in rapid succession—fit, generous, genius. Then put them all together: Witty SBF who loves to cook and see good and bad movies ISO Mensa-minded, athletic, giving SBM. Now add something specific to really grab their attention, such as a quote, pop culture reference, or question—"Wanna catch the next Steven Seagal movie (if there is one)?"

Top off your ad with a catchy headline. Here are a few samples to get your creative juices flowing.

Your Headline:	**What It Indicates:**
Looking for a few good men	Noncommittal
I'm 32 flavors and then some	Confident
Do you give love a bad name?	Challenging
Sports lover	Deferential
Animal lover looking to unleash the tiger within	Cheesy
Do you have your game on?	Confident
Ready for fun?	Sexually adventurous
Can you handle this?	Aggressive
STOP! In the name of love	Clever
More Betty than Wilma	Playful
Meat lover wants to meet lover	Passionate

Picking a Winner

If someone responds to your ad, the only thing you have to go on is his voice and what he says. Voices can be misleading, especially if he's nervous or if there's a lot of noise in the background. However, you can look for a few clues. For instance, is he on a cell phone? Is he in his car, a crowded restaurant, bar, or a quiet place when he calls you? Does he seem breezy and distracted or intense and dead serious? Is he chatty or monosyllabic? Does he use proper grammar and big words, or does he speak poorly and pepper the message with slang? Does he have an accent? If so, can you place it? Is his voice deep or high and reedy? Does he sound smooth or nervous?

Think about this. A bit of nervousness can be charming or irritating. An accent can be devastating or a total turnoff. But his voice should not be a deal-breaker, unless he sounds like a cartoon character or total stoner. His message, however, is another story altogether. What exactly does he say? How can you read between the lines?

What he says:	**What he means:**
You sound sexy.	You sound easy.
I own my own business.	I don't have insurance.
I'm 6 foot, 180 pounds.	I'm 5'8" and weigh 200.
I work out every day.	I'll skip the gym if a good game is on TV.
I wish I could get outside more but I'm so busy...	I'm allergic to pollen.
I have a dog.	My car smells like ass.
I own my own home.	My favorite place is Home Depot.
I work hard and play hard.	I will never let you win at anything.
I have a new sports car or Humvee.	I'm compensating for my physical shortcomings.
I'll treat you like a queen.	I'll buy the first round.
My friends say I'm funny.	I have an extensive *Simpsons* collection on DVD.
I have blue eyes.	I have blue eyes.
I have blond hair.	I used to have blond hair.
I'm really good at darts.	I really need to meet women.
I read a lot of nonfiction.	I read the paper.
I'm a great cook.	I know my way around the grill.

Of course, much of what he tells you is true in whole or in part, but keep in mind that he's trying to make a good first impression. He's going to portray himself in the best light and that might mean stretching the truth a wee bit. But this works both ways and you should feel free to do the same. And if you both know this from the get-go, chances are good that you won't have your high expectations dashed when you finally meet.

His first message will usually include a little information about himself, why he was attracted to your ad, and a number where you can call him back if you're interested.

Taking It to the Telephone

How long should you talk via phone before actually meeting? If you have moved to the phone after responding to a personal or after someone messaged you, take the opportunity to subtly grill him. Ask him questions about his business, family, relationship history, what he wants in future relationships, interests, and so forth. Be careful however not to supply too many details about yourself—maintain your privacy.

Give out your cell phone number and make sure your voicemail doesn't give too much information away. Since personal ads are so brief and anonymous, you need to be more concerned about your safety until you have established enough of a communication and decide to meet.

If you enjoy your phone conversations and want to know more, set up a meeting over coffee or drinks. This clearly indicates that you are meeting for only an hour and you'll be able to get out of the situation quickly, if necessary. This will minimize "damage" if you aren't feeling chemistry in person. And it's fair to convey that to the man after the date. Leave him a message, e-mail him, or tell him over the phone that you enjoyed meeting him but you don't feel that you have a love connection. And then move on.

* Speed Dating

Also known as fast dating, rapid dating, quick dating, etc., speed dating started in Jewish circles as a way to get to know other singles in a "musical chairs" kind of way. A mixer for grown-ups, the same number of men and women pay a fee and register for an event at a local bar or restaurant. Once there, you are given a worksheet and a number. You then chat up a single man for a set period of time, a bell rings, and then you move onto the next man. You keep track of who you'd like to see again on your worksheet. At the evening's end, you turn in your preferences and if there's a match (i.e., a guy you liked likes you too), the organization sends e-mail addresses or phone numbers to the interested parties. After that, you are on your own to see each other as long and as much you see fit. My friends from the U.K. called this event "barbaric," but hey, it's worth a try and you get to move on from anyone who you find boring, cheesy, or smelly without having to come up with a creative excuse.

Here are a few national organizations sponsoring speed dating events; check your local papers or search engines for other events. Pubs, restaurants, and clubs have jumped on the bandwagon and are hosting similar events; in Philadelphia, even the Restaurant School is hosting a speed dating event (which includes a five-course meal).

Pre-Dating

Pre-Dating is a national organization that has events in various cities for different age ranges and sexual orientations. You'll talk to from ten to twelve single men in your age and interest group, through a series of six-minute "pre-dates" at a local bar, café, or restaurant. If there's mutual interest, organizers send you an e-mail with each other's contact info so you can arrange your "first" date. For more information, check out their website at pre-dating.com.

HurryDate

HurryDate parties are held at bars and lounges in cities nationwide. Each party is organized so you'll meet up to twenty-five people via a whirlwind of three-minute dates. After each date you'll circle a "yes" or "no" next to each person's number if you want to see him again. If two people checked "yes," HurryDate sends an e-mail within a few days, listing the first names and e-mail addresses of the people with whom you matched. View cities and events at hurrydate.com.

SpeedDating

SpeedDating is a service for Jewish singles. In one evening, you are guaranteed to meet seven people in one-on-one conversations of seven minutes each. The organization supplies topics to discuss if you need a little help; after each round, you check off whether you'd like to see the person again. If both sides are interested, organizers give each person the other's phone number. For more information and to find out if there is an event in your region, check out aish.com/speeddating.

* Blind Dates

Should you trust your friend's judgment and go out on a blind date? Well, your friends probably know you better than anyone and probably have a good idea of who/what you're looking for. And if a friend is going out on a limb and setting two friends up, she or he usually has a good vibe about it. Often, two friends will have similar personalities or energy levels so it seems clear that they'd get on like a house on fire. Chemistry isn't taken into account but this is a great start.

If you have a friend who is trying to fix you up, suggest that she arrange a group setting (cocktail party, pub crawl, dinner party at a favorite restaurant) or double date in which to meet. You'll have a good support network in place and if conversation lags, your friend can jump in and bail you out.

Play Internet Detective

When you are sniffing out a blind date, do what you can to ferret out as much information about him as possible. In other words, Google him! Use a massive search engine such as Google and type in his name and any other key words you can find. If you only know his first name, you may think there's little to be found out. You'd be wrong! For instance, my friend Josh was set up with a woman named Lana. But he also knew she was a publicist, lived in Chicago, and went to Northwestern University. By typing "Lana," "publicist," "Chicago," and "Northwestern" into Google, he found out where she worked, what year she graduated (he extrapolated her age from this), and even what she thought of the eighties (she was quoted in a story about the eighties revival that was happening when *The Wedding Singer* came out). Okay, this wasn't enough to know if he was going to hit it off with her, but it filled in a picture in his mind's eye and he was much more enthusiastic as the date approached (by the way, it wasn't a love connection but you never know—she might have a friend for him!).

Conversation Starters

I've found that it helps to have a few good questions in your back pocket to pull out should conversation stall or you want to learn more about your date's background, personality, sense of humor, etc. It's also a great way to share some of your more memorable anecdotes. Here's a list of my personal favorites:

What was the first concert you ever went to?

Who would you invite, living or dead, to your perfect dinner party?

If you could have the power of invisibility or flight, which would you choose and why?

What band would you like to see get together for a reunion tour?

If you could be a professional athlete, what sport would you play?

What movie are you embarrassed to love?

What's the cheesiest CD you have in your collection?

Ginger or Mary Ann?

What movie makes you cry like a baby every time?

Who would you recast in a WB remake of *Deliverance*?

Do you have a tattoo? What did you get and where did you get it?

What's the biggest bonehead thing you've ever done?

What's your favorite comic book or cartoon character?

What's the best trip you've taken?

If you could have bionic sight or hearing, which would you choose?

What's the best thing you've ever scammed for free?

Have you ever shoplifted anything?

What magazines do you subscribe to?

What's the last book you read?

Sometimes you really want to know certain details about your date but you don't know how to ask. Here are some polite ways to ask about your date's background early on:

Allergic: Do you have any medical problems I should know about?

Pets: Are you a dog person or a cat person? Do birds freak you out?

Loyalty: Tell me about your oldest friend.

Handy: What's in your toolbox? No, not that toolbox.

Former Boy Scout/in group therapy: Have you ever had to sit in a circle with a group of people?

Can't hold down a job: Do you find the confines of an office environment stifling? What would be your dream job?

Purveyor of porn: Did you see that documentary on porn star Ron Jeremy, a.k.a. the Hedgehog? How does someone like that get a gig making porn movies?

Former cult member: Have your parents ever had to bail/bust you out of some bad situation?

Medicated: What is currently in your medicine cabinet?

Has a record: Have you ever been fingerprinted?

Number of sex partners: How many boxes of condoms do you think you've bought in your life?

Commitmentphobes: How many names are crossed out in your black book?

Kids: Have you been to Chuck E. Cheese recently?

Sometimes you want your date to know a few choice details about yourself but you are loath to brag. Here are a few ways to casually drop information to impress and enchant your date.

Heiress: That Nicky Hilton spoiled my ninth birthday party.

Serious jock: I better get home early. I'm meeting my trainer at six tomorrow morning.

Large cup size: Gosh, I wish I could run five miles every morning like you but jogging is just so hard on my upper body.

High I.Q.: During my graduation speech, my mortarboard would not stay on.

Former teen model: Models these days start so young. My mom wouldn't let me go to Milan until I was eighteen.

Best-selling author: It's so hard to meet people when you're traveling across the country on a book tour.

Climbed Everest: I haven't been this out of breath since I climbed to base camp.

Child actor: I don't get why Todd Bridges and Corey Haim turned out so bad. Look at me—I turned out fine.

Dated Brad Pitt: Brad was into architecture even in the early nineties when he took me to Fallingwater.

Double jointed: My flexibility served me well on the uneven parallel bars.

* A Few More Options

At this point, you've probably realized that there are more opportunities out there to meet and greet men than you thought. And there's more! Yes, in addition to bars, singles clubs, websites, personal ads, dating services, and blind dates, singles events and organizations are sprouting up everywhere.

Social Clubs

In cities all over the country, social clubs are thriving for active singles. One of them, Events & Adventures, has forty to fifty events each month in Seattle and Portland clubs. You can pay a membership fee and then a lower rate for whatever event you want to participate in (kayaking, hiking, billiards, theater-going, for example). Nonmembers can also attend events on a case-by-case basis but they pay a higher fee. Groups also exist in Denver (funindenver.com), New York (socialcircles.com), Chicago, and Minnesota. Check to see if a group has cropped up in your city.

Dating Cafés

In New York City, The Drip Café (dripcafe.com) has books and videos of customers that you can look through. If you like the look of one of the regulars, you can set up a coffee date at the café. You can also set up a profile yourself. With ten affiliates in the New York and New Jersey area and three in Boston, there is sure to be one in your city in the near future.

Matchmakers and Coaches

Well, Hello Dolly! No longer just a movie concept, there are professional matchmakers and social coaches out there working to play cupid and create more satisfying social lives. Robin Gorman Newman is the Love Coach (www.lovecoach.com) and author of *How to Meet a Mensch in New York*. She works with singles to craft a social strategy that fits their lifestyle and personality. Matchmaker Stephanie Daniels runs Samantha's Table (samanthastable.com), which operates like a dating service. Singles in New York and Los Angeles can meet with her in a private consultation and she will then arrange one-on-one drink dates for suitable matches. Keep an eye out for a similar service near you.

Singles Nights

Read your local weekly paper or weekend section of the daily newspaper. Singles nights abound at museums, theaters, restaurants, and coffee shops; this is an excellent opportunity to mill about with a friend until you can zero in on a hottie and chat him up about the event.

I've been told by a woman who owns a dating service that it's better to go by yourself to a bar or singles event. A man is more likely to approach you if you are alone because it's less intimidating than if you're with a friend or in a group. I say this is good advice if you are brave and ooze confidence. However, I think it's best to do whatever is comfortable for you. If you are never going to fly solo, it is a million times better to grab a friend and go out than stay home and pet your cat. And I suspect you won't have to fly solo for long if you are spreading your social wings.

What happens when you do connect with someone and he asks you out? First of all, do a little victory dance. And then start preparing for your first date. The complete date night chapter is only a page away. Get to it.

CHAPTER 5
You've Made Contact!

Right on, sister! You are a living, breathing, swinging single. You are date-worthy (but you already knew that). You are among the dating. Stop for a moment. Isn't this new and fun? The dreamy butterflies and the anticipation of that first touch or kiss drives me mad just thinking about it. Become self-absorbed. Wallow in this feeling, since it only comes around when you are dating someone new that you actually like.

* Before the Date

Create a Persona

Now that you have a date lined up, don't get freaked out. When I set up a date with a man I met on the Internet, I told him that first dates made me nauseous. He wrote back, "Why? You could pretend to be the Queen of Sheba." I liked this comment and I liked him (at least until the second date, that is). This is a very important point. On your first date, you can project the person you want to be. If you are shy, nervous, or know you don't make terrific first impressions but improve on subsequent meetings, try on a new persona. It gives you incredible power and makes you feel in control of the situation.

For instance, I interviewed some dominatrices for a book I was writing last year. After meeting with them, I became more confident when walking on the street because I thought, "For all these passersby know, I could dress up in leather and spank men for money." Thinking that I had a naughty secret life gave me confidence; a mysterious smile played about my lips. I swear, strangers started whistling and saying hi to me. While that might not be the attention you're after, you get my point. Thinking of yourself as a man killer, sex kitten, or just a person who has dated much and often will arm you with confidence and allow you to ease into the date. And don't worry about giving him the wrong impression. Your personality will shine through in good time.

What to Do?

Figuring out what to do on a first date can be a bit irritating. While you may want your date to play cruise director and set up something unique or at least mildly inventive, don't be disappointed if he takes you out for drinks or dinner at an uninspired establishment. He may want to choose a place where he feels comfortable and knows he won't get sick from the food. He may lack imagination. Whatever the case, you may be setting yourself up for disappointment if you don't give him a few cues.

Picking a place where you feel safe and where you know the lay of the land is always a smart idea. You are familiar with the place's exit routes, you won't spend too much time looking over the menu for something to order, and you can relax and focus on your date.

Coffee

If you are on a blind date or aren't sure how you feel about the date, set up a coffee or lunch date. You can pretty much guarantee you can be in and out of there in an hour, hour and a half, tops. You don't have to worry about who's going to pay a hefty tab, and you will avoid distractions while you get to know each other.

Drinks

Meeting for drinks is also a minimal commitment in terms of time and money, but provides the option of moving onto dinner if the date is going well. If you want the date to end when you've drained your martini, simply say you have work to do, you have to call your mom, you are meeting a girlfriend later, or you were out late the previous night and are exhausted.

Dinner, Dinner and a Movie, or Dinner and Drinks

Dinner is perhaps the most traditional first date option but it doesn't have to be boring. Tell him you love Japanese, Thai, Vietnamese, Indian, Ethiopian, or another ethnic cuisine and see if he suggests anything interesting. You can also mention that you heard of a new restaurant that just opened that you've been dying to try. Or perhaps there's a Mediterranean restaurant that features belly dancing on the weekends. This is a great first date, as it provides free entertainment, gives you a topic for discussion, and prevents you from talking (a good thing if the two of you are bashful or not particularly loquacious).

However, don't suggest a restaurant just to be seen in a certain light. For instance, don't say yes to sushi to be seen as adventurous if, in fact, you can only stomach California rolls. If you enjoy your basic continental fare, say so and suggest a fun pub or diner. He'll appreciate that you aren't trying to break the bank.

In my book, a man scores major points if he suggests a place to go. To me, that indicates that he gets out of the house regularly and is, if not worldly, at least plugged into his community. Not to mention, I personally find it very sexy when a man takes charge and is decisive. Yum.

If dinner is followed by drinks or a movie, you must really like each other. You are willing to invest in getting to know your date. Seeing a movie is a double-edged sword. While you don't have to talk to your date for ninety minutes or so, you will have something to discuss afterward. On the other hand, it also places you in a darkened space in close proximity to your date. I think you can safely maneuver the issue of sharing popcorn and other concession snacks, but do you share the armrest, do you allow him to put his arm around you, do you snuggle up to him? As Sandy says to Danny Zuko in *Grease,* "Feel your way." If you are attracted to your date, by all means hold hands, wrestle for control of the armrest, or let him sling his arm around you. It gets cold in the theater and this has the added benefit of warming you up. However, if you are not comfortable with public displays of affection just yet, use your hand closest to him to hold your drink or sneeze into it when he's going for a handhold. He'll get the message. As far as the arm drape, tell him that you are uncomfortable or hold your body rigidly until he pulls away.

My friend Lizzy made the fatal mistake of going out for an Italian dinner with her date before seeing *Josie and the Pussycats*. While her movie choice was suspect, this was not the primary issue. With a belly full of risotto, her date proceeded to fall asleep and snore, much to her chagrin and the derision of other moviegoers. She woke him up twice, only to hear him fall back into the land of nod. The lesson? Don't go to the movies after dining on a rich meal and do not take your date to see a movie marketed to teenage girls. It won't hold his attention and the next thing you know, you'll have a narcoleptic date and/or you'll have to reciprocate by seeing a Vin Diesel movie during your next outing to the multiplex.

Unconventional Date

I give a guy major approval if he proposes an activity off the beaten track. On the third date, an ER doctor took me to an outdoor concert and brought chairs, insect repellant, binoculars, drinks, and a dinner of tuna steaks, shrimp cocktail, and potato salad. At the end of the date, he even bought me a signed CD of the performers I especially liked. Hmmm, why did I stop seeing him?

However, if you are high maintenance (and it's okay to admit it) or have a hard time being spontaneous, you may want to opt for a setting in which you have more control. It ended up raining during the aforementioned concert. I got soaked and my hair lost any resemblance to Kate Beckinsale's coif in *Serendipity.* I was a good sport, however, and I think I earned high marks for my ability to roll with the punches. Or maybe he just liked the effect of my wet T-shirt...

What to Wear?

This seems like a trivial question but believe me, a little forethought will pay off on your date. Regardless of what I suggest, what your friends lend you, or what you just bought at the mall, the overriding rule here is that you be comfortable, both physically and mentally. The last thing you want to think about on a date is how much your feet hurt in your four-inch gladiator stilettos. If you are uncomfortable highlighting your buxom, by all means reach for your favorite turtleneck—you know, the one that matches your eyes—and skip the plunging V-neck sweater your rail-thin friend is forcing on you.

Think about the venue. Where is he taking you? Will you be standing or sitting? If you are going to be on your feet all night, skip the heels and wear a miniskirt if your legs go on for miles. If you will be sitting down for dinner, opt for the A-line dress and skip your designer jeans with the unforgiving waistband. Will you be walking a lot? Wear your swingy skirt and the espadrilles you've had for six years. Will you just be seen from the waist up? Work your outfit around that amazing vintage necklace your mother gave you. Take care not to look too studied or put together. After all, you don't want to look like you're trying too hard. That should be *his* job.

Form-fitting jeans and a nice sweater or blouse are acceptable in most venues (barring Michelin-rated restaurants or weddings, of course), but here are a few suggestions for some traditional and unconventional date destinations.

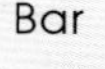

Bar

Considerations: You could be standing or sitting. If sitting, you could be on a high stool at the bar or in a booth.

What to wear: Pretty much whatever you want. The bar, depending on its vibe (see Chapter Two for a breakdown of bars) is the place to be either dressy or casual so wear what you feel and look good in.

Coffee shop or Café

Considerations: Sitting in a booth or at a table. Focus on your outfit from the waist up.

What to wear: This is a laid-back date intended to be low pressure. Wear jeans or comfy trousers and a sweater—preferably knit from a luxury fiber like cashmere—with little to no jewelry. Keep your makeup to a minimum; throw on a yummy lip gloss and enjoy the conversation along with your skim decaf gigante almond latte. Make sure you lick away the extra foam on your upper lip.

Concert

Considerations: You could well be standing for all or part of the evening.

What to wear: Slip on comfortable shoes that have been broken in. Add your best blue jeans, a trendy top, jacket (you may get cold or heated up as the concert rages on), and a small shoulder bag (skip the bag if you can get away with it).

Jazz club

Considerations: You'll be sitting around a small table in this refined, dim atmosphere.

What to wear: Since lighting will be low, you can break out something a bit more colorful and be more dramatic with your makeup. A long skirt and high-heeled boots or shoes will blend in perfectly with the vibe of the club.

Movie

Considerations: Well, you'll be in the dark for two hours.

What to wear: Something tactile that he can brush up against in the dark! Velvet, leather, cashmere, mohair, angora, or faux fur are all delectable choices. As far as what kind of garments to wear, really anything goes except formal wear.

Beach

Considerations: Do you want to go into the water? If you spent an hour on your hair and don't want to get dunked in the surf, try to avoid the beach as an initial date spot. You'll just be seen as a bad sport.

What to wear: A bathing suit if you are comfortable showing off your bod. Shorts and a T-shirt or an exotic pareo draped creatively over your body will tease him and leave him wanting more. Don't forget the sunscreen and a floppy hat.

Hiking

Considerations: Well, duh, you are going to be outside and you are going to be walking.

What to wear: T-shirt, flannel shirt or jacket, old jeans or cargo shorts, wool socks, hiking boots, butt pack to store water, sunscreen, and the all-important trail mix.

Kite Flying or Frisbee

Considerations: Need to be able to move and get dirty.

What to wear: Grubby clothes, such as overalls and a boy-sized T-shirt, and pigtails. Free your inner child!

Gallery or Museum

Considerations: You'll be strolling about the room slowly. You'll want to both fit in and stand out.

What to wear: Always bet on black. Sleek. Minimalist. Highlight one great piece of jewelry, such as a gigantic ring that looks like a satellite dish.

Diner Dinner

Considerations: You'll be playing footsie in a booth. Make your mark from the waist up.

What to wear: Be a bit quirky and let your inner hipster out. Wear an oversized men's blazer or your brother's mint-condition Members Only jacket. Wear a fedora low on your head as you wash your chili burger down with a black-and-white milk shake.

Ethnic Restaurant

Considerations: You'll be sitting in a chair or maybe even on a cushion.

What to wear: Get creative with your accessories. Wear a peasant blouse and those earrings your roommate brought back from her Peace Corps stint in Niger.

Fine Dining

Considerations: The atmosphere will be elegant and you'll want to look like you were born to eat pâté.

What to wear: Dress to the nines. March out your most elegant cocktail dress, sweep your hair into an updo, swipe on crimson lipstick, and slip into your most daring stilettos.

Dancing

Considerations: Think J-Lo, not John Travolta. Bare skin seems to rule the day at the dance club. To make sure you can dance like a maniac, maniac on the floor in your ensemble, don't constrict your arms, legs, or ribcage.

What to wear: Think hot, hot, hot (see Chapter Two). Short swingy skirts with shimmery lotion on your legs is a sexy combo. Low-cut and/or sleeveless tops are smokin', and don't forget about your favorite dancing shoes.

Wedding

Considerations: You'll be doing pretty much everything during a wedding ceremony and ensuing reception. Note of caution: Do not invite a man to a wedding if you've only been dating him a short while, especially if you are a member of the wedding party. He'll feel as if he's being presented to your friends and family as your significant other and he probably won't know many people at the event. Avoid the risk, fly solo, and flirt with the single men at your table.

What to wear: Get your game on. Wear the fabulous daring dress you've been hiding in your closet for a year. Strap on your beaded kitten heels. Why should the bride be the only one in the spotlight?

Making Up Is Hard to Do

Now that you've got your ensemble figured out, take extra care with your hair and makeup. In my experience, there are two features that men never fail to fall for: "natural" lips and loose, sexy hair. It's often said that men like woman to wear little to no makeup and I have indeed found that to be true in some of my boyfriends. Yes, they don't want to wake up next to someone who bears little to no resemblance to the vampy vixen they went out with the night before.

But I've also dated men who appreciated the touch of drama I brought to my appearance on occasion. And what men think is a "no makeup" look might just be very artfully applied makeup (Bless them, they aren't always the sharpest tack in the box, are they?). So if you are addicted to mascara, eyeliner, blush, concealer, foundation, lip gloss, or lipstick, go for it. You'll feel more comfortable and confident facing your date with the makeup you normally wear. I would recommend a "less-is-more" approach, however; avoid makeup that will rub off on his collar, look too obvious, or stain his skin.

As for creating beguiling lips and hair: Men like lips to look immensely kissable, which for me means filling my lips in with a nude lip liner a shade deeper than my real color and topping it with a similarly colored lip balm or gloss. My lips look soft and shiny, a bit bee-stung, and immensely kissable. Couple your perfect pout with hair that is also soft and shiny and swings. Trust me: He will start thinking about running his fingers through your hair and/or how soft your locks will feel brushing against his skin. Avoid hair that looks like it took thirty minutes to create, has a lot of product or pins in it, or is obviously a "hairdo." If a guy is afraid his hand is going to get stuck in your updo, he's not going to go near it. And that's a shame.

Packing Your Handbag

While you may be wanting to bust out your new Isabella Fiore clutch or Coast wristlet, resist the temptation and carry a reasonably sized bag when on a date. In addition to serving as a bludgeoning weapon should your date get fresh, you can also pack some essentials. Believe me, when you start sweating through your silk blouse, you'll be happy you tucked a sample-sized deodorant in your bag.

But if you have created a whole snappy ensemble around your precious bag, I'm not going to hold you back. Go for it. Look cute but be tactical when packing it. Like a Girl Scout, you should be prepared for anything, whether you are hiking in the woods, doing needlepoint, or in your case, navigating through a date.

Clutch Essentials

- Cell phone
- Lipstick
- Powder and/or blotting papers
- Keys
- Cash (at least enough for cab fare)
- Credit card(s)
- I.D.
- Tissue
- Condom(s)
- Tampon(s) (if it's that time of the month)
- Medication (if you need it or think you might want to self-medicate by the evening's end)
- Lollipop (for a quirky prop or if your blood sugar gets low)

Handbag Essentials

- All of the above, including:
- Mirror
- Any other makeup item you rely on, such as mascara, blush, concealer, or eye shadow.
- Nail file
- Comb
- Sample-size deodorant
- Hand lotion
- Breath freshener, mints, strips
- Sunglasses and sunscreen (if it's a daytime rendezvous)

Totebag Essentials

- All of the above, including:
- Hairbrush
- Umbrella
- Nail polish (for repairs or stocking runs)
- Hairspray
- Change of underwear, facial cleanser, and moisturizer (in case of a sleepover)
- Sweater
- Earplugs (if he's boring or he snores)
- Handcuffs (you never know, right?)
- Pepper spray or personal safety alarm
- Membership cards to organizations he admires
- Crossword puzzle, half completed
- A book you know will impress him, bookmarked and well worn

- A notebook and pen to write down your impressions of the date or to slip the cute waiter your phone number.

The Date

The Pick-up: Be Smart

So it's not romantic. So what? Thinking about your safety early on will allow you to relax and concentrate on your date as the evening progresses.

When going out with someone who's an unknown quantity (blind date, Internet match, pickup from a bar) versus someone you've known for a while or who has been recommended by a mutual friend, take extra care and do not be too quick to trust him. Many women, including myself, jump the gun if they have a generally good impression of a guy. They allow their date to drive them home and they give them details about their life, including employer, phone number, every e-mail address they have, etc. In doing this too soon, you are making yourself vulnerable and making the relationship harder to break off if he isn't the guy for you. Value yourself and your personal information and dole it out slowly and with purpose. And it doesn't hurt to keep an air of mystery about you!

Here's a few basic dos and don'ts.

- Do meet him at the site of the date. Don't let him pick you up at your home.
- Do set up an e-mail account under a fake name. Don't give him your work e-mail address.
- Do give him your cell phone number. Don't give out your home phone.
- Do let friends know the details of your date and when you expect to be home. Do not allow your date to change the location of your meeting at the last minute. Don't allow him to take you to another place if you are uncomfortable or are unfamiliar with the establishment.
- Do carry a cell phone. Don't meet him at a place that is dark or unpopulated.
- Do allow him to hail a taxi for you. Don't get in a car with him.

While thinking about safety does have a tendency to kill the mood, it's certainly better than ending up harmed in some way. Be careful.

Keep Chivalry Alive

Let your guy have a chance to show off his gentlemanly behavior. Let him hold the door open or the chair out for you. Notice if he lets you order first, if he orders for you (after getting your input, of course), if he's prompt, if he notices that your drink is low, and if he pays the bill. None of these actions are essential but

courtesy and good manners go a long way. How he takes care of you is a small indication of whether he cares enough to make a good impression.

But that doesn't mean you should be a passive participant in the date. Ask him questions about himself. This is a great chance to explore his likes, dislikes, hobbies, career aspirations, etc. Ask whatever you want, but know that men often appreciate witty banter initially. It breaks the ice and know that if there's chemistry, there will be subsequent dates to discover his sexual history or his position on having children or the current administration. If you need a little help in clever conversation, check out the conversation starters in Chapter Four (see page 65).

Foods to Eat on a First Date

Men like woman to have a healthy appetite. I always think of Angelina Jolie doing an interview early in her career while eating a plate of ribs. Men may not like their women overweight, but they certainly like a little meat on the bone. So whatever you eat, eat with gusto.

Sushi: Sexy, baby. Order small rolls that you can eat in one bite.

Finger food, pupu platter, shrimp cocktail: This will keep the focus on your mouth.

Salmon, tuna, sea bass, swordfish, mahi mahi: Easy to cut and an excellent source of protein.

Mashed potatoes: Shows you are real and aren't focusing on your weight.

French fries: Finger food and potatoes—what could be better?

Steak frites: You are passionate about life and red meat.

Pork chop: Very tidy.

Chocolate: A sensual way to end an evening.

Potpie, shepherd's pie, soufflé, frittata, but not quiche: All the food groups are represented in one yummy concoction.

Crepes: Oh la la.

Stir fry: Showcases your healthy side.

Ceviche: This zesty seafood dish shows your adventurous side.

Oysters: The classic aphrodisiac (just make sure they're from a reliable source).

Fondue: You can share and it's just so indulgent.

Small-sized pasta, such as penne or gnocchi: No errant sauce will find its way onto your clothes.

Crab cakes: Easy to wrangle onto a fork.

Family-style portions of anything: If you can find dishes to share, it's a great way to encourage intimacy.

Foods to Avoid on a First Date

A big salad: It's just so cliché.

Beans: Duh.

Chili: See above.

Spaghetti: It is a danger to scarves, blouses, and dignity.

Garlic: Okay only if your date orders it, too.

Beets: They stain your teeth and your clothes.

Lobster: Unless it is taken out of the shell, you can look pretty unattractive trying to wrestle the meat from the claws or body.

Double-decker sandwiches: Don't order

anything that cannot fit into your mouth easily.

Chicken or duck on the bone: Beyond the breast and thigh, it is awkward to cut.

Cooked cabbage: It is a gas producer.

Ribs: While it's sexy to eat with your fingers, you'll get stuff stuck in your teeth.

Pesto: This also gets stuck in your teeth.

Fishy-smelling fish: Again, duh.

The Issue of Going Dutch

It's pretty simple. If he asks you out, he should pay but it's nice to offer assistance. I usually say, "Can I help you out with that?" If he says yes to this, I'll file it away on my mental checklist, along with any other decidedly ungallant behavior he's displayed that evening. But if you ask him out, you should pay. If he insists on paying regardless, let him and thank him kindly.

✳ The End of the Date

So the date is coming to a close and your normal confident self has gone out the window. How, exactly, do you seal the deal? Do you want to seal it with a kiss or do you want to drive that final nail in the coffin? Do you linger in the car or at the door, or do you thank him nicely and bolt? There are a lot of cues to recognize and techniques to employ but don't overthink the situation. Just promise you'll do one thing: Follow your gut. Instinct is a powerful tool and if you are feeling massive attraction to your date and you get the feeling he's a stand-up guy, let him kiss you or grab hold of his face and plant one on him.

How do you go for it? Maybe he's reluctant to make the first move or you are just feeling the need to plant one on him. Either way, there's absolutely no reason why you can't kiss him first. While he may be a bit surprised, if you have both been clearly having a good time, the kiss will not be unwelcome. Men often love it when women know what they want so thank him for a lovely date, lean in, and kiss him softly on the lips. If he's receptive, kiss him as long and as deeply as you like. However, I wouldn't recommend moving in on any other areas of his body at first. Feel him out figuratively before feeling him out literally!

However, if your attraction is battling with a vague unease, tell him you had a nice time and end the date with a kiss on the cheek or a squeeze on the arm. That's not to say you shouldn't go out with him again but just be cautious. And if you aren't attracted to him but he seems like a great guy, be friendly but end the date. If he asks to see you again, be honest. Tell him that you think he's great but you don't feel the chemistry. Maybe you can parlay your date into a friendship; he might even be perfect for one of your friends!

If he doesn't try to kiss you or ask to see you again, play it cool. He may be nervous and resurface by e-mail or phone in the days following the date. If he simply isn't interested, you probably won't hear from him again and you should look elsewhere for someone who will be more appreciative of what you have to offer.

At the end of the date, play it safe. If you are hopping in your car, get your key out and insert it into the car lock. Once inside your car, wave at him as you lock the door, strap on your seatbelt, and rev up the engine. If you are not sure if he is trustworthy, end the date a few blocks away and prevent him from seeing the make and license plate of your car. If you are hailing a cab, allow him to flag one down for you and make your goodbye brief. If you are walking home, make sure he doesn't follow you and walk in a well-lit populated area. Take a circuitous route home if you suspect he might want to find out your address. If you allow him to drive you home, make sure your car door is unlocked, so you can make a clean getaway. (Before you go out, turn on a porch light.) He should see that you get safely inside. When you unlock your door, turn and wave.

To Kiss or Not to Kiss?

There is no hard and fast rule about kissing on the first date. I have friends who think it's unseemly to kiss before date #3. One girlfriend of mine is completely turned off if a guy tries to kiss her right away, no matter how great the date is. She thinks it too forward. I don't share this view. I've kissed and been kissed by men on the first date and it was completely appropriate

and at other times, completely disgusting. But that had to do with age, technique, and how much I liked or loathed the guy. So I go with the flow.

I had a fantastic time with a doctoral candidate named Tim on our first date. I was tipsy, he hailed me a cab, and I kissed him without thinking (which is completely unlike me). When I later broke down the evening, I couldn't believe myself but on the other hand, I still think it the most spontaneous thing I've done on a first date. Happily, he e-mailed me the next morning at 7:30. He felt the same way about me and I think I knew this and was in a comfort zone when I laid one on him.

If you are kissing him in public, don't prolong it. Giving someone the tongue in public is unseemly and you might want to save the passionate kisses for when you are alone. However, a quick kiss can definitely convey your receptiveness and serve as a promise of more to come. If you want to get away kiss-free, claim that you are uncomfortable with public displays of affection and politely thank him for the date. He might get the drift if you have a touch of sang-froid about you.

Sex on the First Date: Yes or No?

Uh, no. Promise me you won't do this (or more accurately, him), unless you are just looking for one night of sex. If you like him, prolong the anticipation and let the courtship bloom. Don't blow your wad, so to speak, at once. Foreplay and buildup are so utterly delicious, why would you want to skip over them?

Even if you are just looking for one night of sex, it most likely won't be very good, seeing as you have not achieved any level of intimacy. In my experience, sleeping with someone right away does not result in a lasting relationship. Of course, having a satisfying sexual experience is another story.

Well then, when, you might ask? There's no hard and fast rule. I've held out for months and I gave it up on the third or fourth date. It's instinct. It's the level of trust you have in him. It's a great leap of faith to jump in the sack with someone and you have to be sure that he's not going to hurt you physically or emotionally. Do you think he may brag to his friends that he bagged you after two weeks of dating? If so, you probably want to get to know him a little better and feel more comfortable before pursuing a sexual relationship with him. And you know that you can satisfy men in so many ways these days that going all the way isn't all that necessary for him. And if a man becomes increasingly impatient or insistent on having sexual relations with you, you may want to reconsider a relationship with him. If he is not willing to go at a pace comfortable for you, that may not be a relationship worth pursuing.

On the other hand, you may love intercourse and want to satisfy your sexual cravings right away. And you may not be looking for a long-term relationship with one guy. You may enjoy playing the field and having many sexual partners, either in rapid succession or in rotation. You go, girl! Just do not let your libido get the best of you. Keep a healthy supply of condoms on hand and act responsibly. Being single has a lot of perks, and varied sex is definitely one of them. And putting out no longer means that a guy is going to lose interest. Some men are only interested in making a conquest but the "Why buy the cow when you can have the milk for free?" theory is a thing of the past. Moo!

* His Place or Yours?

When you are having sex for the first time, you may very well not care where the heck you end up as long as it's nearby. However, there are advantages to luring him to your place, as well as getting busy at his pad. And it can be made really special by taking it on the road and visiting a hotel, motel, bed & breakfast, inn, cabin, or backseat. Here are a few considerations for having sex at your place versus his place.

Your place:

You know when the sheets were last changed.

You control the lighting concept.

You wake your neighbors.

You see how he reacts to your pet.

You have to hide your dirty laundry, not to mention stuffed animals.

He checks out your lame CD collection.

He uses your bathroom as much and as long as he wants.

He spies an unflattering childhood photo of you.

He meets your hot roommate.

He discovers your obsessive-compulsive disorder.

He realizes you have a black thumb.

You can kick him out in the morning.

His place:

You get to spy.

He lets you into his fortress of solitude.

You watch postcoital digital cable on his big-screen TV.

He waits on you.

You check out his CD collection.

You do not have your products with you (unless you tote samples in your handbag).

You can't take your contacts out.

You listen to him take an early-morning call from his mother.

You determine if he's familiar with Soft Scrub, Comet, or anything with scrubbing bubbles.

He can give you the boot in the morning, claiming an early meeting.

The Follow-Through

Beware Your Stalker Tendencies

If you had what you thought was a magical date with someone and you don't hear from him, it's natural to wonder what the heck happened or if you just imagined the chemistry. Don't fret. Don't obsess. In all likelihood, you both felt the chemistry but life got in the way. He may not have called for many reasons—he moved, he was still nursing a broken heart, his self-esteem was low, he found out he had an STD and was horrified, he lost your number (lame but I suppose this could still happen, as guys don't seem to be aware of the phone book or directory assistance), or in the case of my friend Natasha, he unexpectedly became a father.

In other words, it may not be about you at all. So don't let his lack of response get you down. Feel free to send him one follow-up e-mail and if he doesn't jump at the bait, cut your emotional line to him. You've got other fish to fry. And believe me, they will be very tasty.

A Few Dating Dos

- Do let him pamper you, woo you, shower you with gifts.
- Do let him drive or walk you home and pick you up (after the first few dates that is).
- Do let him hold the door or chair for you.
- Do allow him his space/let him go underground for a few days.
- Do let him go out with his friends.
- Do let him pay.
- Do let him see the real you—wearing no makeup, an emotional mess, a jeans and T-shirt kind of girl, etc.
- Do struggle to see the real him, not who you'd like him to be.
- Do go on with your own life.
- Do listen to your instinct.

A Few Dating Don'ts

- Don't take him shopping with you.
- Don't show him all facets of you right away.
- Don't fill up your dance card with him every night.
- Don't assume he'll pay but do let him.
- Don't call him or e-mail incessantly if he doesn't call you after promising to. Give up.
- Don't start talking about marriage or commitment on the first, second, or third dates.
- Don't be available for last-minute dates.
- Don't think you can change him or try to.
- Don't lend him money or give him keys to your car or home.
- Don't knit, crochet, throw, weave, paint, sculpt, or make him a gift of any sort. In knitting circles, it's bad luck to knit a gift for a man you are dating. There are all sorts of theories about why this is: He feels obligated to reciprocate, he hates it and thinks you don't know him at all, he adds up the hours you spent making something for him and gets freaked out, he thinks it's a physical manifestation of commitment. Whatever the case, it's prudent to avoid bestowing gifts on him early on. Let him woo you and just sit back and enjoy it.

Warning Signs You Should Get Out Immediately

These little gems have been culled from my own dating experiences, as well as from a few dating mishaps that involved my friends. It's amazing how naturally these rolled off the top of the head.

- He refuses to see a foreign film.
- He refuses to see anything *but* a foreign film.

- He invites you out for brunch, agrees to let you split the bill, pockets your cash, and then charges the entire amount while you are in the bathroom.
- In the flesh, he bears absolutely no resemblance to his Internet photo.
- He makes excuses as to why he was late, why he didn't call, or why he forgot the date.
- He shows up late to the date with a crease on his face, because he had fallen asleep an hour before.
- He shows up thirty-eight minutes late to the date because he was looking for street parking (when parking garages are on every corner).
- The first time he kisses you, he has gum in his mouth.
- He hasn't been to the dentist in five years.
- He says he's been looking for someone just like you...two hours into the first date.
- He bores you on the first date. Believe me, it doesn't get better.
- He takes you to a music festival to see his ex-girlfriend perform.
- He edits your sentences or fixes your grammar.
- He really wants to go back to your place on the first date, even though you said no.
- He thinks no means maybe.
- He picks you up in his parent's car...and he's thirty-two.
- He lives in the basement of his parent's house...and he's thirty-seven.
- His mom deposits his paychecks.
- He kisses a man in front of you on New Year's Eve (yep, this really happened to me).
- He flirts shamelessly with other women in front of you.
- He looks at your chest when talking to you.
- He doesn't walk you home.
- He takes you to see a slasher flick on your first date.
- He keeps trying to make you eat a burger, even though you're a vegetarian.

- He answers every cell phone call, regardless of where he is.
- He heads straight for the porn section of the video store.
- He starts with the sexual innuendo way too early on.
- He sets up shop in your bathroom...if you get my drift.
- He was once in a Moonie colony.
- He wears a huge class ring with a simulated sapphire on his ring finger.
- He's mean to your cat.
- He has small hands.
- He has an aversion to deodorant.

- He doesn't own a TV and thinks anyone who watches television is dumb.
- He doesn't give you his home phone number.
- He has a growing collection of Hummel figurines.
- He inventories his Hummel figurines.
- He calls you while he's on the toilet...and tells you.
- He wears bad shoes.
- He only wants to eat at T.G.I. Fridays.
- He leaves you at the table for a fierce game of darts.
- He introduces you to his parents on the third date.
- He sleeps in a sleigh bed.

Okay, admittedly, some of these things are fixable or silly but if something about a guy doesn't ring true to you, listen to yourself and respect your instinct. What may seem like a trivial thing, like wearing too much product in his hair, might actually point to a deeper problem, such as vanity and hubris.

Keeping Your Cool

If you do get on with your date and want to see him again, remember not be too keen during the early stages of a relationship. This means limiting his access to you and making sure you are not instantly available whenever he calls. I'm not talking about following any rigid rules; just do not make everything in your life suddenly revolve around him and when you can see him. If you automatically clear your dance card for him early on, he's going to think you have no life and are becoming dependent on him for your social life and happiness. This may scare him off even if he's been the one pursuing you and asking you out five times a week. I dated a guy who immediately started calling me his girl, introducing me to his friends, and calling me up for impromptu dates. Things progressed rapidly and after six weeks, he sent me an e-mail (he was also a coward) telling me that he wanted to slow things down. After giving him a verbal tongue-lashing for his mixed signals (which he admitted even though it didn't change anything), the relationship deteriorated. If I had been less accessible, I wonder how long the relationship would have lasted beyond that.

So remember to keep cool and don't lose your head after a few dates. Don't feel the need to call him every night before bed. Limit your dates to a couple of times a week at first. Don't instant message him as soon as you get online. Don't tell him what your coworkers think of him when he hasn't met them yet. Don't invite him out to happy hour with your friends until you are sure everyone can play it cool. In other words, tread cautiously, and don't introduce him to your mother until you've passed the six-month mark. The issue of pacing and developing the relationship is dealt with in more detail in the next chapter.

To end on a more positive note, there are obviously many, many reasons to continue dating one or several promising young men. You don't have to limit yourself to dating just one guy so try and keep your options open until you feel ready to make a firm commitment, if that's what you want. Make sure you stay open minded about the guys you date. A great kisser with a good heart can make you forget all about his massive collection of Star Wars memorabilia. He just becomes quirky or endearing because overall, he's a great guy. So keep kissing that boy and let's move on to the adventures that face you in the world of going steady!

CHAPTER 6
The Next Step: Going Steady

If you've made it this far, it probably means that you're happily dating someone. Hurray! While some issues have gone by the wayside—like feeling the pressure to go out and flirt and "be on" all the time—other issues are going to crop up. Being aware that relationships take work and vigilance will ensure that you have a successful go of it.

Pacing is critical. I've been in relationships where we were both immediately comfortable with each other and fell into happy coupledom. But this is rare and runs the risk of taking each other for granted or assuming that you understand each other completely when you may still need to be in the "getting to know you" stage. So take your time finding out more about your guy and establishing a comfort level that works for both of you.

How do you do this without playing games, you ask? It's not as hard or manipulative as it seems. Just live your life. Before he came along, you had a career and friends and a social life and intellectual pursuits. (At least, I hope so.) While it's tempting to drop activities to make room for him—and you'll definitely want to go underground with him for the first few weeks or months while you're in your honeymoon/lust phase—don't do it. Friends will feel blown off, your work may suffer, and you may at some point feel as if you sacrificed part of your personality or life for him. You may feel that you let the world pass you by while you spoon with your guy.

Also most guys really do like women who have a full life already. It takes the pressure off them to "be your everything" (to quote the Bee Gees). Instead of feeling trapped (a common feeling amongst the wily male), they will feel the need to perform and pursue. And believe me, you want to prolong this as long as possible because once it's gone, it's usually gone forever (with the exception of key holidays).

Exclusivity

When do you actually verbalize that you're both ready to quit the dating scene and focus solely on each other? This is tricky but necessary. If you don't sit down and talk about your feelings and relationship, you may have different assumptions. You might think that since you're obviously besotted with each other and spend all your free time together and he's told you that you're the funniest/loveliest/kindest/sexiest woman he's ever dated that it's clear that you are "going steady." Au contraire! He might be amazed that he has such a sweet situation with you. You are so much fun and you don't seem to care that he's still Internet dating or seeing other chicks. You haven't asked him so you must not care, right? "Don't ask, don't tell" and all that. So talk! It doesn't have to be somber and portentous. Here's a sample script to work from. Improvise or embellish as you see fit.

YOU: Hey [name or pet name], I've been having so much fun with you these past [insert weeks/months]. It seems as if you feel the same.

HIM [nodding]: Of course I do, baby! You're the best thing since [insert major invention or his favorite football team]!

YOU: Well, I am kind of at that place where I don't want to see anyone else. After all, where would I find the time? What are your thoughts on just dating each other?

HIM: I thought you'd never ask!

Actually, his response might be more along the lines of, "Well, um, gee, I hadn't thought about it. Um, okay." He may want to think about it or he may be reluctant. If this is the case, you may want to express to him that you are looking for one special guy and you think he may be it. If he's not looking for a serious relationship, you may have to move on, even though you really dig him. This isn't a threat to get him to pony up some commitment; you're just being honest and clear about your romantic goals. If he does feel the same as you—fantastic. You are going steady, girl!

Feel Your Way

When you meet the right guy, it should be crystal clear how quickly things should move and what action you should take. Rules go out the window. If your gut tells you this is the one (or at least a one), go for it and throw conventional behavior out the window. However, you may need some pointers to get you over some typical stumbling blocks.

My friend Jane dated a man for a few weeks. Things intensified very quickly. She was giddy over her guy. He met her friends and received their seal of approval. But Jane opted out of inviting him over to her mom's house with other friends for a birthday dinner. Even though her mom was too cool for school, there was too much pressure surrounding meeting a parent so soon into the relationship. Well played, Jane!

However, another's zeal can overshadow your own good sense. It happens to the best of us. It happened to me. One of my former paramours gave me the full-court press within the first week of dating. He called me his girl, he took care of me when I came down with the flu. I let him. I was flattered and lulled into believing that he was falling for me. Actually, I think he was. However (you knew there had to be a "however," didn't you?), as much as he liked me, the fear of a new relationship was greater. After a couple of months of giving me signals and signs that he wanted to fill the role of boyfriend in the drama of my life, he slowed things down. But it was too late; I broke things off.

Then there's the issue of saying "I love you." When is the right time and should you wait for him to pony up the words first? In the case of my friend Carrie, she dated Kevin for a year. They had both been damaged by previous relationships and it took a long period of casual dating before they started to get serious and exclusive. Then their love exploded and they became inseparable! Carrie realized she was head over heels in love and decided to tell Kevin. She felt a deep level of trust and connection with him. She needed to get it out and let him know how much he meant to her. She actually told him that she didn't want him to respond to what she was telling him. She just wanted him to listen and accept her love. He did feel the same but it took him a few months to spit it out. Meanwhile, Carrie wasn't sweating it because giving the gift of her love was more important that receiving his at that time. Besides, she felt his love, even if he couldn't come right out and say it.

Meeting the Parents

In a new relationship, the issue of meeting his friends and relatives is always tricky and depends completely on how comfortable you feel about it. I had a guy take me to meet his parents within two weeks of dating. That should have tipped me off and sent warning flares shooting into the sky, but, well, I was young and romantic. Meeting the parents is not to be taken lightly! Relationships are hard enough without bringing key relations into the picture right away. I think it's lovely to talk to your parents about your current guy and for him to talk to his family about you. That definitely means he is interested in pursuing a long-term relationship with you.

But parents yield a tremendous influence, no matter how old your date is or how long he's been living on his own. A mother's seal of approval or frown of disapproval lodges in the back of your man's brain and

can subtly or unconsciously influence his actions, if not his feelings. Establish a solid relationship with your guy before meeting the parents or introducing him to yours. Make sure you are over the moon about him and that you have both agreed to date each other exclusively. Don't assume this is the case. If it's not verbalized, you may have different assumptions about the relationship. Once you feel that this guy could be the one (or at least "a" one), pony up the parents and enjoy the experience. Don't act too familiar; call them Mr. or Mrs. until they give you the go-ahead to assume a first-name basis. Compliment their home, play with their pets, and give them a firm handshake and take their lead on more intimate greetings (like a hug or kiss on the cheek). Try to keep the suck-up within you in check.

Navigating the Holidays

Dating is hard enough without taking holidays and special events into consideration. New Year's Eve may be icky when you are flying solo but it can be even more disastrous if you push togetherness before you've put in the time. He'll read "serious relationship" into the situation, even if all you want is a pair of lips to kiss at midnight. However, that said, there are no hard-and-fast rules, and if the relationship is going well, you probably should expect something. If you know you'll be disappointed if the holiday comes and goes and he didn't do anything and you didn't say anything, play cruise director and set something up with your guy if you think he'll be receptive.

In my opinion, here's what you can reasonably expect on the following days:

Valentine's Day

Two weeks: Nothing. Don't bring it up. Make plans with your girlfriends and avoid the day altogether. If he brings it up or brings you a gift, be surprised and thank him kindly. You'll reel him in with your nonchalance.

Three months: If you've been dating for a few months, it's reasonable to expect a small gesture and a date on Valentine's Day. Flowers and a dinner date is the combination that a good guy will bring to the table three months in. If he doesn't, he may not be on the same page as you.

Six-plus months: Expect flowers and/or dinner. If he's got his game on, you may also be surprised by a nicer gift, like earrings or a getaway to a bed & breakfast.

Thanksgiving

Two weeks: Spend it with your family and call him from home. Don't expect to spend this family-oriented holiday with him.

Three months: Tough call. You can invite him to dinner at a friend's house or suggest cooking dinner together, but it's still too early to bring him home and introduce him to the family.

Six-plus months: If he's met your parents already, bring him home with you. This can be a stressful holiday laden with implications so it's better to ease him into your family dynamic before you start carving turkey or watching football.

Christmas

Two weeks: Expect to trade holiday greetings and maybe a Christmas card. This is often considered a family affair so he may go underground to avoid the situation and because he's spending time with his family and reverting to childhood.

Three months: Expect to score a modest nonintimate gift of a CD or book.

Six-plus months: There are no hard and fast rules but you should be able to count on a nice gift of jewelry or spa gift certificate, or something you had on your Christmas list.

New Year's Eve

Two weeks: Nothing. Don't mention it.

Three months: Make plans together. This is the time to be out smooching with the one you're dating. This is not a night he can ignore or blow off.

Six-plus months: You should both be planning this night together, be it dinner and movies in or a fancy party at the top of a tall building. Revel in your coupleness and enjoy the night.

Your Birthday

Two weeks: He probably won't give you a present but he may want to take you out to dinner for your birthday. If you aren't sure about him yet, don't mention that it's your birthday and make plans with your pals instead. You want to guarantee a fun night, after all.

Three months: A gift and/or flowers and/or dinner. He'll know how casually or seriously to treat the event, based on how much you've discussed it. It helps to give him some ideas of how you'd like to spend the day.

Six-plus months: A gift and flowers and dinner. He should be ready and willing to treat you like a queen for a day.

His Birthday

Two weeks: Wish him a happy birthday and promise to buy him a drink the next time you go out.

Three months: Give him a modest gift and take him out to his favorite restaurant. Reward him with some nookie.

Six-plus months: Open the door naked and have him unwrap his gift in bed while you unwrap him. Okay, that may be a bit saucy so invite a few of his favorite people out for a dinner party and give him his gift (tickets to his favorite sporting event are always, without fail, guaranteed to be appreciated) when the two of you are alone.

Do you feel fully prepared to sustain a healthy, measured, romantic, sizzling relationship? Good—let's get to the juicy stuff!

The Bedroom and Beyond

Finally, we are getting to the good stuff! Sex is hard enough without thinking about the details. A little forethought will allow you to relax and discover a few new erogenous zones. Regardless of what you call it—making whoopee, making love, intercourse, knockin' boots, or doing the deed—sex is tricky. We are trusting someone to see our private and vulnerable parts. And vice versa. And you know what? It's hard to talk about frankly.

It took me years to free myself of my decorum and delicacy regarding such matters and now I can talk with relative ease about sex toys, positions, unexpected delights and disappointments (if you get my drift), and orgasms. And I've learned that like snowflakes, no two sexual experiences or partners are ever alike. There are no tips I can give you that are guaranteed to make a man your eternal love slave. Every guy is different; nibbling on one man's ear might send him to the moon whereas going for a lobe on a new boy might make him feel like he's getting a tongue bath. And we don't want that!

The one piece of advice that I can offer is to explore your guy's erogenous zones as well as the things that you think might give you pleasure. Push yourself to reach new heights. Just because something feels really, really good doesn't mean that it can't feel even better.

✳ Setting the Mood

A little bit of predate prep will set the stage for an evening of good lovin' at your place. Have a lighting concept, complete with candles, planned out. Have your stereo loaded with songs of seduction. Have some key snacks stocked in the pantry or refrigerator. Make sure your house is clean or, at the very least, that dirty laundry is stuffed in a hamper and surface clutter is artfully hidden. Check that your sheets are up to snuff (or sniff, as the case may be).

Lighting

If you have a three-way light switch or dimmer, lighting is a snap. Dim the lights, especially around your bed, couch, floor, or designated area of nookie. Have a couple of candles strategically placed (make sure you've burned them previously so it's not obvious from the wick that you brought out the candles just for him) so a gentle flame can cast interesting shadows and flickers over your bodies and the walls. If you have found a particularly appealing scented candle, by all means light it. However, take care not to mix scents, overpower the room with too many of the same scented candle, or drive him away with a strong feminine scent like rose (instead, choose an earthy, musky, or citrus smell).

Bed and Other Designated Love Zones

Chuck the stuffed animals and flowery sheets. You want your date to feel comfortable and if he's swathed in Laura Ashley floral sheets, he's going to feel a little girly rather than like the virile, strapping example of manhood you've convinced him he is. Load up your bed (couch, floor, etc.) with pillows and throw pillows. With a down comforter, chenille throw, and other tactile bedding, he'll never want to leave your cozy love nest. Just keep your beloved stuffed Smurfette out of sight.

Food for Foreplay

While it's not your job to feed your date, you may find yourself hungry when you get to your place or you may need refreshments after your physical exertions. Here are a few ideas of snacks to have on hand:

Really good chocolate, such as Toblerone, Godiva, or Lindt.

Nuts—they provide protein and can be easily grabbed with a free hand.

Grapes, strawberries, or other finger fruits—cleaned and ready for eating.

A good dessert item, such as cake, pie, or cupcakes

Sugary kids' cereal, such as Cap'n Crunch or Cocoa Puffs

Ice cream (skip the nonfat frozen yogurt). Hand him his own spoon and eat directly out of the pint or carton.

Forego crunchy foodstuffs, such as cookies and potato chips, which will leave behind crumbs. As far as beverages go, always keep a bottle of champagne cooling in your refrigerator, alongside a six-pack of bottled microbrew beer. Keep caffeinated soda and a good bottle of both red and white wine on hand.

Mood Music

When setting the stage for a satisfying romp, don't forget to pick some sexy tunes. I'd avoid playing a mix CD; it may suggest too much forethought. However, there are some great soundtracks and CD options that will put just about anyone in the mood for love. Here are a few favorites culled from my and friends' collections:

- India Arie, *Acoustic Soul*
- Erykah Badu, *Baduizm*
- John Coltrane and Johnny Hartman, *John Coltrane with Johnny Hartman*
- Coldplay, *A Rush of Blood to the Head*
- Ry Cooder and Ali Farka Toure, *Talking Timbuktu*
- D'Angelo, *Voodoo*
- Miles Davis, *Kind of Blue*
- Deep Forest, *Pure Moods*
- The Delfonics, *La-La Means I Love You: The Definitive Collection*
- Bob Dylan, *Live 1966 Royal Albert Hall*

- Enigma, *Love Sensuality Devotion: The Greatest Hits*
- Marvin Gaye, *Sexual Healing*
- Stan Getz and Joao Gilberto, *Getz/Gilberto*
- David Gray, *White Ladder*
- Al Green, *Greatest Hits*
- Billie Holiday, *Songs of Lost Love*
- The Inkspots, *Java Jive*
- Janet Jackson, *The Velvet Rope*
- Norah Jones, *Come Away with Me*
- Lenny Kravitz, *Lenny Kravitz Greatest Hits*
- Massive Attack, *Mezzanine*
- Massive Attack, *Protection*
- John Mayer, *Room for Squares*
- Moby, *Play*
- Morcheeba, *Who Can You Trust?*
- Morphine, *The Night*
- Willie Nelson, *Teatro*
- Les Nubians, *Princesses Nubiennes*
- The Pixies, *Bossanova*
- Portishead, *Portishead*
- *Round Midnight* soundtrack
- Roxy Music, *Avalon*
- Sade, *Love Deluxe*
- Sade, *Lover's Rock*
- Jill Scott, *Who Is Jill Scott?*
- Andres Segovia, *The Romantic Guitar*
- Sting, *Nothing Like the Sun*
- Zero 7, *Simple Things*
- Anything by Ella Fitzgerald, Etta James, or Prince

✳ Focus on Foreplay

Some women can orgasm by just having a few lustful thoughts. Most of us, however, need a helping hand. You already know how great it feels to build and prolong pleasure. I don't have to explain this to you. However, I would encourage you to explore your own body and discover new erogenous zones (which can change depending on your lover and his unique touch.) Do you like a light, feathery touch? Do you prefer a firmer hand? Do your nipples virtually vibrate when stimulated or is it the base of your spine that sends you?

Once you know your pleasure points, show him the way! He isn't a mind reader and we often fall in the trap of thinking, "If he knows me so well, he should be able to figure out what I like." Men are indeed magical creatures but they aren't always psychic or skilled in the art of loving ladies. So give him verbal cues. Moan when you like something. Better yet, be direct. Say things like "Yes, I love that," or "Don't stop," or "That feels great." And show him the way. Take his hand and place it where you want it. Keep your hand over his and apply pressure or move his hand as you school him in your body. He will be an apt and attentive pupil, methinks.

* In the (Erogenous) Zone

Every body and every man is different but here's a guide to the most delicious erogenous zones and a few ideas on what to do when you find your mouth or fingers straying into that region.

Earlobes: Gently tug on them with your teeth. Dart your tongue into his ear. Blow softly in his ear. Beware of ear wax!

Neck: Lightly stroke his neck with the backs of your fingers. Plant butterfly kisses on the sides of his neck. Avoid giving a hickey!

Adam's apple: Lap at his Adam's apple with long strokes of the tongue.

Nipples: Tread carefully here. Men can be very skittish if you go anywhere near their nipples. However, that said, some men find it very erotic to have their nipples manipulated. Kiss the area, suck on the nipples, gently tug on them or the hair around them.

Fingers: Slowly suck on each one. Massage between the fingers and all the way from the base to the fingertips. Knead the meaty area between his thumb and fingers.

Chest: Rub your hand over his fur.

Stomach: Softly blow on his stomach and stroke it lightly with your fingertips.

Sacral area (where the buttocks meet the spine): In my experience, this convergence of nerve endings is a magical spot for men. Massage this area firmly with your thumbs and you'll have him—figuratively and literally—in the palm of your hand. The buttocks and backs of the thighs are pretty good areas to explore in this same manner.

Toes: Check them out first (if the lights are low, save toe action for another time). If they seem groomed and odor free, surprise him with a reflexology massage. To really make him see stars, suck on each toe in turn while massaging or stroking the rest of the foot.

* Orgasms and the Promised Land

First of all, if you are feeling good, that is all that matters. If you cannot reach orgasm easily or at all, don't worry. Pressure and stress will only further inhibit your ability to feel yummy.

I had a friend in college who couldn't reach orgasm. Her boyfriend—I swear—told her that something was wrong with her. In retrospect, this was a simple case of a man feeling inadequate about his own prowess but, at the time, my friend was devastated. As you can imagine, she didn't have a good sexual experience until she dropped her boyfriend and found someone willing to invest the time and energy to draw out her elusive orgasm (let's face it, all that stroking and nibbling and kissing and rubbing is not for the faint of heart or those sad souls on a tight schedule).

And that brings me to another point about which I feel very strongly: Don't fake it! Faking an orgasm only succeeds in making your partner think he's doing everything right. How on earth are you ever going to climax if he thinks he's satisfying you and you are thinking how to moan and writhe and curl your toes in a convincing fashion? If you are concentrating on your acting skills, you are probably not focusing on relaxing and letting yourself go. You are just perpetuating a cycle of little or limited sexual pleasure. In other words, you are only hurting yourself.

The next time you are tempted to fake it because you are exhausted, starting to chafe, or can't breathe under his weight, try instead tapping him on the shoulder and telling him to stop.

Don't be afraid of being honest. Believe me, a man would rather know what you like and get a little direction than do something you hate that you will most likely describe in detail to your girlfriends later. The fear of humiliation is much, much greater than the fear of being schooled between the sheets. He figures that as long as he has you in bed, it's all good, even if you have a few helpful pointers for him.

* Disappointed in His Body?

The answer is obvious: Turn off the lights! Actually, odds are that there will be something you don't like about his body—an unexpected but massive tattoo, untamed body hair, love handles, badly situated mole, etc. If you like him and his technique, then work with him. Hopefully, you will be over the moon about this guy and your rose-colored glasses will be on. If not, try these ways to embrace (literally or figuratively) his entire body. Remember it's not what you have, it's what you can do with it that counts!

Visualization: Imagine that his tattoo gives him special powers. Think of his slender penis as a divining rod, finding the wellspring of your pleasure. Visualizing parts of him in unconventional ways will only fuel your imagination and turn a perceived negative into a positive. Embrace the enemy: Play with his body hair by pulling on it or twisting it. Use body paints and play connect-the-dots with his freckles. Whatever the physical attribute, find a way to have fun with it or to incorporate it into your foreplay. You'll have fond memories of it the next time it's staring you in the face. Hide it: If all else fails, encourage him to wear socks to bed if his feet are crusty. Substitute candles for overhead lighting. Think about how kind and giving he is, close your eyes, and relax.

* Morning Sex, Quickies, Afternoon Delight, The Great Outdoors

Mmm, there's no better way to wake up than to someone rubbing or kissing you in all the right places. But of course, there are things like a full bladder and morning breath to contend with. If you get a chance to slip into the bathroom and do a bit of repair work, or at least empty your bladder and swig some mouthwash, do it. You'll be much more comfortable, even if you momentarily kill the spontaneity of the moment. It won't take a minute to resume activities.

If you have only a few minutes to get down and dirty, don't waste precious minutes removing all of your clothing. Just pull down or push up the obstacles to your key areas and get to it. I'd suggest a basic, tried-and-true position, such as missionary or woman on top; now is not the time to get creative. You just need to satisfy your animal urge and focusing on the essential naughty bits will make you feel a bit dirty and primal.

If you have the opportunity to avoid responsibility and loll around in bed all afternoon, do it. You may decide to make this a weekly or monthly ritual. Take your time. Explore each other's bodies. Giggle. Nap with your backs to each other. Make him paint your toes. Draw the blinds. Not only will the privacy render you completely uninhibited, the soft light of the sun will filter into your room and cast a warm glow over the room. If it happens to be raining, listen to a combination of raindrops and soft R&B as you hunker down under the covers.

If you are taking your act on the road, namely outside, there are a few things to consider. Make sure you pack a blanket, water, snacks, tissues, and condoms (not only for safety but to avoid any residual messiness). Scout out the area to make sure people and critters are not afoot. Check the weather report—you don't want to be caught in a thunderstorm when you were planning on a short hike followed by a long sexcapade. Of course, if the mood strikes you while you are out for a stroll, limit your activities to a clandestine make-out or grope session. I was once making out with a boyfriend against a tree in a wildish area of Colonial Williamsburg when some adolescent boys happened upon us. We inadvertently put on a show but it wasn't anything for which we were going to be arrested or that would permanently scar the boys.

Birth Control

You may not want to deal with the mechanics surrounding sex but, well, you have to. You have to protect yourself against an unwanted pregnancy and sexually transmitted diseases or infections (STDs, STIs). Here's a list of the various methods of contraception (ask your physician for further information regarding any birth control medication you are interested in using).

- Abstinence
- Tubal Sterilization, Vasectomy
- Condom
- Diaphragms and Cervical Caps
- Female Condom

- Spermicide
- The Pill
- Lunelle: The Shot
- Norplant: The Implant
- Depo-Provera: The Shot
- Ortho Evra: The Patch
- NuvaRing: The Ring
- IUDs

✻ A Few Tips for Satisfying Sex

- Do use protection!
- Don't do anything you are uncomfortable with or dislike.
- Do give him positive reinforcement.
- Don't expect him to talk after sex. He needs time to collect his thoughts or he just may be tuckered out.
- Do feel free to send him home after sex.
- Don't expect to spend the night, or have him spend the night at your place.
- Do explore his body.
- Don't be shy.
- Do ask him to perform oral sex on you.
- Don't expect him to reciprocate after you've performed oral sex.
- Do feel free to tire him out.
- Don't be coerced into sex if you are tired, hungry, or just not in the mood.

* Less than Great Sex

If at first you don't succeed, try, try again. Seriously, it can take many passes at sex before sex is satisfying to both parties. Show and tell him what you like. Give him verbal reinforcement when he's doing something right. Take your time with foreplay so that you are aroused before intercourse. If you like someone enough to have sex with him, it's worth a little effort and time to see if you can improve upon it.

* In the Light of Day

Okay, you did it. You know, it. Sex. Now what? You probably were focused on getting it on, not to mention stressed about doing it for the first time with your new man. So you probably haven't given too much thought to the aftermath. Depending on your actions at this critical juncture, you can have the outcome you desire, whether that means you never want to see him or his ratty apartment again or you can't wait for round two, three, and beyond.

You had unbelievable sex.

Yippee! Revel in your postcoital glow. Give a trusted confidante a blow-by-blow account. Get some rest. After all, if it was good for you, it was most likely good for him as well. And it won't be long before he's knockin' on your door, ready to knock boots again.

Rather than giving into the urge to call, e-mail, or unexpectedly drop in on him soon after your sexcapade, try to play it cool. Leave him wanting more. When he calls or e-mails, wait a few hours before responding. While I don't prescribe to any set rules, a little restraint will drive home the point that you're a rare commodity that he would do well to invest in and snap up.

The sex was just okay. You're willing to give him another try.

This is probably the most common scenario unless you've happened to be unbelievably lucky up to now. He may be over the moon about your night together and not realize that you don't feel the same. This isn't a good sign. He may not be listening to you or intuiting your feelings. He may just be self-absorbed. But for your encore presentation, give him an opportunity to rise to the occasion, so to speak. Show or tell him what you like. Work to find a pace that's comfortable for you. If you don't communicate with him, chances are that things won't improve.

The sex was not okay. You feel icky, can't wait to shower, let alone get away from him.

Bummer. First of all, are you sure it won't get better? Is his technique terrible? Is he coachable? If you can't go there or picture him in the buff ever again, take him off the hook and throw him back into the water. There are ways to do this gracefully and be clear. I suggest gently telling him that you just don't feel the chemistry is there and that, while you enjoyed meeting him, you don't think you see a future with him. Of course, he may feel exactly the same way. He may beat you to the punch and tell you something similar or just not call you. Don't be hurt by his rejection. Breathe a sigh of relief that you got out emotionally unscathed.

Here are a few scenarios that might happen to you the day after your first throw down:

You slink home alone on the walk of shame.

Are you beating a hasty retreat from his place after a night of slightly embarrassing behavior brought on by too much booze? I think you are focusing on the wrong things. Remember: You just had sex, sister! Lift your bed head, put a spring into your step, and look passersby in the eye with your raccoon eyes. You are a saucy siren! Women want to be you, men want to be with you. After all, you got some. Wear it like a badge of honor as you work your way home. Stop for a huge breakfast. Don't worry that your panties were lost somewhere between his hallway and sofa. Whether or not you see him again, enjoy the slightly tired, slightly giddy feeling of recent sex.

He is ready for round two...and maybe three.

The question is, are you? Was it good for you? Have you had enough? Or are you ready to see him in the light of day. If you are ready for a little morning nookie, go for it! Just don't get too carried away that you forget about getting to work on time or about that breakfast you set up with your mom. This all still counts as the first time between the sheets so don't worry about appearing too eager. This is a great time to check out his body in the sober light of day. You can also take this opportunity to show him a few things you like that you didn't have a chance to introduce in the previous evening's frenzy.

He wants to have breakfast.

Go for it. Eat with gusto. Let him pay. Or if it was really, really good, pick up the check and thank him. He's done enough for you. Don't count on spending the next morning or day with your guy after a night of passionate intimacy. He may just need some time to regroup or be by himself. He may get up and start working at 6:30 every day. Don't take it personally. Resist the temptation to run out and get bagels and coffee for the two of you. As lovely as that sounds, he may think you're presumptuous or that you have overstayed your welcome. Leave him wanting more.

If you are hungry and feel your blood sugar level getting low, tell him you need to get going if you are at his place. If you are at your apartment, tell him you're famished and slip out of bed and fix yourself a snack. Offer him a bite. That said, look for cues. While he may be anxious to get started with the rest of his day, he may very well want to keep the date going. Maybe all your physical exertions have made him hungry and he'll suggest going out to his favorite diner for a small snack with a side of home fries. Let him make you something since he keeps boasting about his perfect omelet or mastery in the kitchen. Here's to a lifetime of breakfasts in bed!

He makes excuses and is out the door in a flash.

Well, um, there may be a viable reason for this but men I know say if the sex is good, there's nothing on his schedule that can't be delayed for a few hours. He's either freaked out by the idea of a relationship and commitment or he just isn't interested in anything beyond your night together. Either way, you may want to consider moving on. Obsessing about him and trying to figure out what he's thinking and feeling will get you nowhere.

But see how he follows up in the day or days following your tryst. He may need time to process what an unbelievable time he had with you. If his follow-up is good, give him another chance. If he displays the same behavior, talk to him about it and see what he says. I dated a guy who woke up every day at 6 A.M. without fail. He would start worrying about his Ph.D. dissertation and future job prospects. He would get antsy and/or depressed, and have to leave. This made me feel pretty

lousy time after time and eventually I realized that his personality and behavior were fixed. So I had to give him up in order to find someone who'd want to watch the Food Network or MTV with me all morning.

He says he'll call or makes vague promises of seeing you again.

Don't hold your breath. He may have just seen you as a conquest but more likely, he's just not feeling the chemistry. Like above, you may want to move on to greener, more promising pastures if you don't hear from him within a week.

He calls you as soon as you walk in the door (or has left you several messages already).

Beware. He may truly be besotted with you but he may also be desperate to be part of a twosome and you are the likely candidate to fill the slot of girlfriend. It is important to keep momentum going if you've been having a great time. But really think about how you feel about him; don't be led into a relationship you aren't ready for because he's so taken with you.

While it may seem soon to you, if he's coming on strong, you may want to have a "relationship talk" with him. Ask him what he's looking for and what he wants out of a relationship. If it jives with your desires, great. Just tell him you need him to respect your pacing. If his thoughts are radically different from yours, tell him that you aren't ready for such a relationship and gently break it off.

He calls after ten days and wants to get together that same night.

Having sex for the first time isn't to be taken lightly. If he's treating it and you capriciously and you feel it was more important to you, tell him. He may not be able to think very far in advance. Test him by calling him up at the last minute and suggesting a date for that night. If he's game, then it may be that he's just a poor planner. Tell him you need a bit more structure and advance notice—after all, you're a busy girl—and have him meet you halfway (i.e., setting up a date a day or two in advance).

But if his lack of consideration stems from relationship skittishness, you need to take more drastic measures. If you allow him to be breezy at this point, you may be establishing patterns that will continue if the relationship progresses. I dated a guy who never put out any effort. I had to visit him, only go to places where he was comfortable (i.e. the bowling alley and T.G.I. Fridays), and accept his quirks. It was my own fault because I allowed this to happen over and over. Make him value you, your time, and your intimacy. Don't go out with him on the spur of the moment. Don't allow him to call every now and

again for a hook-up if that's not cool with you. That said, you don't have to play games either. Just temper your enthusiasm for him with healthy doses of self-worth and self-preservation.

He doesn't call.

He is doing his best to drive home the point that guys suck. After one call or e-mail, leave him in your rear-view mirror.

Looking Good the Day After

If you find yourself at his place after a night of nookie, it's a snap to soothe whisker burn and repair displaced makeup if you have access to his bathroom. Grab whatever gear you have, slink into the bathroom, and assess the damage. Open the curtains or blinds. Natural light may be unforgiving but, at this point, necessary. Is your skin blotchy? Is there residual makeup? Are your eyes red? Do you have bed head? Do you smell, um, ripe?

Never fear. Start by repeatedly splashing cold water on your face. This will invigorate your complexion, remove trace evidence, and, duh, wake you up. If eye drops are not handy, cup your hand, fill it with water, and give yourself a makeshift eye bath. Hold a cold wash-

cloth over your eyes for a couple of minutes. If there's a tube of Preparation H in the medicine cabinet, pat a bit under the eyes for an immediate lift. For an errant zit, a bit of toothpaste will dry it right up.

Tame your bed head. If you have a short 'do, grab some conditioner from the shower, rub a dime-sized dollop between your palms, and apply sparingly to the hair like a gel, tousling it ever so slightly. It works, and not in a *There's Something About Mary* way. If your hair is longer, sleek it back into a ponytail (dental floss will work in lieu of a rubber band).

Dry lips and other flaky patches can be soothed with a bit of Vaseline. It also makes your eyelashes especially glossy. (Don't stop to question why the jumbo tub of petroleum jelly is holding court on the back of the toilet). Put some toothpaste on your index finger and finger-brush your teeth.

If you reek, do not apply perfume. That's way too French. Take a damp washcloth and give yourself a sponge bath in key areas, using a dollop of shampoo in lieu of bar soap. Air dry or towel yourself off. Stuff your unmentionables in your bag and go commando. Rifle through the medicine cabinet for any absorbent powder. (If you are sufficiently awake at this point, check out prescriptions bottles to see if he's heavily medicated or recently suffered a nasty rash.) At this point, you are definitely ready for round two—unless you think he isn't looking or smelling so good in the light of day.

* Conclusion

Now you're fully briefed on the dating scene and equipped to take it by storm. You know how to find your man, how to hook him in with the right pick-up lines, and how to secure that important first date. You are an expert at making a great impression on potential suitors, from how you talk to how you dress. Now that you have all of this sort of information tucked away, you are free to make eye contact with that tall drink of water across the room. You are ready to place an ad in the newspaper or post an Internet profile. You are ready to get your dating game on! Happy dating!